ALL-IN-ONE
Student Workbook
Version A

2013
Edition

Prentice Hall

Course 2
MATHEMATICS
Common Core

D1254198

Taken from:

Prentice Hall Mathematics, Course 2, All-in-One Workbook, Version A

PEARSON

Front Cover: Paul Frankian/Index Stock Imagery, Inc.
Back Cover: Corbis/Picture Quest

Taken from:
Prentice Hall Mathematics Course 2: ALL-IN-ONE Student Workbook Version A, Global Edition
by Randall I. Charles, Mark Illingworth, Bonnie McNemar, Darwin Mills, Alma Ramirez and Andy Reeves
Copyright © 2010 by Pearson Education, Inc.
Published by Prentice Hall
Upper Saddle River, New Jersey 07458

Pearson Learning Solutions, 501 Boylston Street, Suite 900, Boston, MA 02116
A Pearson Education Company
www.pearsoned.com

Printed in the United States of America

6 7 8 9 10   V011 17 16 15 14 13

000200010271665669

SD

ISBN 10: 1-256-73689-9
ISBN 13: 978-1-256-73689-9

Daily Notetaking Guide

Practice, Guided Problem Solving, Vocabulary

Chapter 1: Integers and Rational Numbers

Chapter 2: Equations

Chapter 3: Inequalities

Chapter 4: Ratios, Rates, and Proportions

Chapter 5: Percents

Chapter 6: Geometry and Area

Chapter 7: Surface Area and Volume

Chapter 8: Analyzing Data

Chapter 9: Probability

A Note to the Student:

This section of your workbook contains notetaking pages for each lesson in your student edition. They are structured to help you take effective notes in class. They will also serve as a study guide as you prepare for tests and quizzes.

Lesson 1-1

Comparing and Ordering Integers

Lesson Objective	Common Core Standard
To compare and order integers and to find and add opposites	The Number System: 7.NS.1.b

Vocabulary

Integers are _____

_____

_____

Two numbers are opposites if _____

_____

_____

Example

① Finding an Opposite Find the opposite of 2.

The opposite of 2 is ☐ , because 2 and ☐ are each ☐ units

from ☐ , but in ☐ directions.

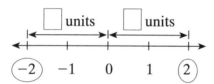

Quick Check

1. Find the opposite of each number.

    a. −8   **b.** 13   **c.** −22

Examples

❷ **Adding Opposites** What is the sum of −5 plus 5?

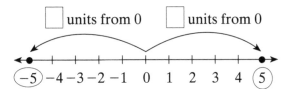

☐ units from 0   ☐ units from 0

−5 and ☐ are ☐, so they are additive inverses.

The sum of additive inverses is always ☐.

−5 + 5 = ☐

❸ **Comparing Integers** Compare 3 and −8 using <, =, or >.

−8 is ☐ units to the left of 0.   3 is ☐ units to the right of 0.

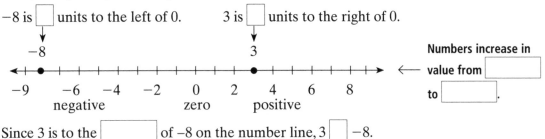

Numbers increase in

← value from ☐

to ☐.

Since 3 is to the ☐ of −8 on the number line, 3 ☐ −8.

Quick Check

2. Find the sum.

   a. 8 + −8   **b.** 3 + 3   **c.** −5 + 5

3. Compare −8 and −2 using <, =, or >.

Name _____ Class _____ Date _____

Lesson 1-2   Adding and Subtracting Integers

Lesson Objective	Common Core Standards
To add and subtract integers and to solve problems involving integers	The Number System: 7.NS.1.a, 7.NS.1.b, 7.NS.1.c, 7.NS.1.d

Vocabulary and Key Concepts

Adding Integers

Start at zero. Move to the first integer. Find the ☐ of the second integer and move that distance.

If the second integer is

- Positive: move in the ☐ direction (right).
- Negative: move in the ☐ direction (left).

Examples $3 + 5 =$ ☐ $-3 + (-5) =$ ☐

Subtracting Integers

To subtract an integer, add its ☐.

Examples $3 - 5 = 3 + ($☐$) =$ ☐ $-3 - 5 = -3 + ($☐$) =$ ☐

Two numbers are additive inverses if _____

_____

Example

1 **Adding Integers With a Number Line** Use a number line to find the sum $-4 + (-2)$.

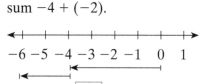

Start at ☐. Move 4 units ☐.
Then move another 2 units ☐.

The sum is ☐.

Quick Check

1. Use a number line to find each sum.

$-8\ -7\ -6\ -5\ -4\ -3\ -2\ -1\ \ 0$

a. $-8 + 1$ **b.** $-1 + (-7)$ **c.** $-6 + 6$

☐   ☐   ☐

Name _____ Class _____ Date _____

Examples

❷ **Adding Integers** Find $24 + (-6)$.

$|24| = \boxed{}$ and $|-6| = \boxed{}$ ← Find the absolute value of each integer.

$24 - \boxed{} = \boxed{}$ ← Subtract $\boxed{}$ from 24 because $|-6| \boxed{} |24|$.

$24 + (-6) = \boxed{}$ ← The sum has the same sign as $\boxed{}$.

❸ **Subtracting Integers** Find $-7 - 2$.

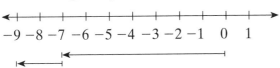

$-9 \ -8 \ -7 \ -6 \ -5 \ -4 \ -3 \ -2 \ -1 \quad 0 \quad 1$

Start at $\boxed{}$. Move 7 units left.

← Then $\boxed{}$ the opposite of 2,

which is $\boxed{}$.

$-7 - 2 = -7 \boxed{} (-2) = \boxed{}$

❹ **Application: Weather** Recorded temperatures at Amundsen-Scott Station in Antarctica have ranged from a low of $-89°F$ to a high of $-13°F$. Find the difference in temperatures.

Subtract to find the difference.

$-13 - (-89) = -13 + \boxed{}$ ← Add the $\boxed{}$ of -89, which is $\boxed{}$.

$ = \boxed{}$ ← Simplify.

The difference in temperatures is $\boxed{}$.

Quick Check

2. Find each sum.

    a. $-97 + (-65)$ **b.** $21 + (-39)$ **c.** $22 + (-22)$

3. Find $-6 - 1$.

4. During the biggest drop of the Mean Streak roller coaster in Ohio, your altitude changes by -155 ft. The Texas Giant™ in Texas has a -137 ft change. How much farther do you drop on the Mean Streak?

Name _____ Class _____ Date _____

Lesson 1-3   **Multiplying and Dividing Integers**

Lesson Objective	Common Core Standards
To multiply and divide integers and to solve problems involving integers	The Number System: 7.NS.2, 7.NS.2.a, 7.NS.2.b

Key Concepts

Multiplying Integers

The product of two integers with the same sign is [___].

Examples $3(2) = $ [ ] $-3(-2) = $ [ ]

The product of two integers with different signs is [___].

Examples $-3(2) = $ [ ] $-3(-2) = $ [ ]

Dividing Integers

The quotient of two integers with the same sign is [___].

Examples $10 \div 2 = $ [ ] $-10 \div (-2) = $ [ ]

The quotient of two integers with different signs is [___].

Examples $-10 \div 2 = $ [ ] $-10 \div (-2) = $ [ ]

Example

❶ **Multiplying Integers** Find each product.

a. $3(7) = $ [ ] ← [___] signs; [___] product. → **b.** $-3(-7) = $ [ ]

c. $3(-7) = $ [ ] ← [___] signs; [___] product. → **d.** $-3(7) = $ [ ]

Quick Check

1. Simplify the expression $-4(-7)$.

[   ]

Example

❷ **Dividing Integers** You are riding your bicycle at a speed of 12 ft/s. Four seconds later, you come to a complete stop. Find the acceleration of your bicycle.

$$\text{acceleration} = \frac{\text{final velocity} - \text{initial velocity}}{\text{time}}$$

$$= \frac{\boxed{} - \boxed{}}{\boxed{}}$$

← Substitute ☐ for final velocity, ☐ for initial velocity, and ☐ for time.

$$= \frac{\boxed{}}{\boxed{}} = \boxed{}$$

← Simplify. The ☐ sign means the bicycle is slowing.

The bicycle's acceleration is ☐ ft/s per second.

Quick Check

2. Find the vertical speed of a climber who goes from an elevation of 8,120 feet to an elevation of 6,548 feet in three hours.

Lesson 1-4

Fractions and Decimals

Lesson Objective	Common Core Standards
To convert between fractions and decimals	The Number System: 7.NS.2.d Expressions and Equations: 7.EE.3

Vocabulary

A terminating decimal is _____

_____

A repeating decimal is _____

_____

Examples

❶ Writing a Terminating Decimal The total amount of rainfall yesterday was reported as $\frac{1}{4}$ in. Write this fraction as a decimal.

$$\frac{1}{4} \text{ or } 1 \div 4 = 4)\overline{1.00}$$ ← quotient

$$-\square$$
$$\overline{20}$$
$$-20$$
$$\overline{0}$$ ← The remainder is 0.

So $\frac{1}{4} = \boxed{}$. The total amount of rainfall as a decimal is $\boxed{}$ in.

❷ Writing a Repeating Decimal Write $\frac{7}{15}$ as a decimal.

Method 1: Paper and Pencil

← The digit 6 repeats.

$$\frac{7}{15} \text{ or } 7 \div 15 = 15)\overline{7.0000}$$
$$-60$$
$$\overline{100}$$
$$-90$$
$$\overline{\square}$$ ← There will always be a remainder of $\boxed{}$.

So $\frac{7}{15} = \boxed{}$.

Method 2: Calculator

7 ÷ 15 = $\boxed{}$

❸ Writing a Decimal as a Fraction Write 4.105 as a fraction in simplest form

Since $0.105 = \dfrac{105}{1000}$, $4.105 = \boxed{}\dfrac{\boxed{}}{\boxed{}}$.

$4\dfrac{105}{1000} = 4\dfrac{105 \div \boxed{}}{1{,}000 \div \boxed{}}$ ← **Use the GCF to write the fraction in simplest form.**

$= \boxed{}\dfrac{\boxed{}}{\boxed{}}$

❹ Ordering Fractions and Decimals: Surveys In a survey of next year's seventh-grade students, 0.25 said they will come to school by bus, $\dfrac{5}{24}$ said they will walk, 0.375 said they will come in a car, and $\dfrac{1}{16}$ said they will ride their bicycles. Order the means of transportation from most used to least used.

walk $\quad \dfrac{5}{24} = \boxed{}$

bicycles $\quad \dfrac{1}{16} = \boxed{}$ $\left.\right\}$ ← **Rewrite the fractions as decimals.**

Since $0.375\ \boxed{}\ 0.25\ \boxed{}\ 0.208\ \boxed{}\ 0.0625$, the means of transportation are

$\boxed{}$, $\boxed{}$, $\boxed{}$, and $\boxed{}$.

Quick Check

1. The fraction of nitrogen in a chemical sample is $\dfrac{5}{8}$. Write the fraction as a decimal.

$\boxed{}$

2. Write $\dfrac{5}{9}$ as a decimal.

$\boxed{}$

3. Write each decimal as a mixed number in simplest form.

   a. 1.364   **b.** 2.48   **c.** 3.6

$\boxed{}$ $\boxed{}$ $\boxed{}$

4. In a survey about pets, $\dfrac{2}{5}$ of the students prefer cats, 0.33 prefer dogs, $\dfrac{3}{25}$ prefer birds, and 0.15 prefer fish. List the choices in order of preference.

Lesson 1-5   **Rational Numbers**

Lesson Objective	Common Core Standards
To compare and order rational numbers	The Number System 7.NS.2.b, 7.NS.2.d

Vocabulary

A rational number is _____

_____

Example

1 **Comparing Rational Numbers** Compare $-\frac{1}{4}$ and $-\frac{3}{8}$.

Method 1

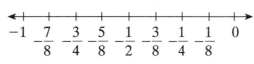

$\leftarrow$ Since $-\frac{3}{8}$ is farther to the

   [   ] on the number line,

   it is the [   ] number.

So, $-\frac{1}{4}$ [   ] $-\frac{3}{8}$.

Method 2

$-\frac{1}{4} = \frac{-1}{4}$ $\leftarrow$ Rewrite $-\frac{1}{4}$ with -1 in the numerator.

$= \frac{-1 \times \square}{4 \times \square}$ $\leftarrow$ The LCD is $\square$. Write an equivalent fraction.

$= \frac{-2}{8} = \frac{2}{8}$ $\leftarrow$ The fraction $-\frac{2}{8}$ is equivalent to $-\frac{2}{8}$.

Since $-\frac{2}{8}$ [   ] $-\frac{3}{8}$, $-\frac{1}{4}$ [   ] $-\frac{3}{8}$.

Quick Check

1. Compare $-\frac{2}{3}$ and $-\frac{1}{6}$. Use $<$, $=$ or $>$.

Examples

❷ Comparing Decimals Compare. Use $<$, $=$, or $>$.

a. 8.7 and 8.1

8.7 ▢ 8.1 ← **Both numbers are positive. Compare the digits.**

b. −8.7 and 8.1

−8.7 ▢ 8.1 ← **Any negative number is less than a positive number.**

c. −8.7 and −8.1

Place the decimals on a
← number line and compare
their locations.

−8.7 ▢ 8.1

❸ Ordering Rational Numbers Which list shows the numbers
$-\frac{3}{5}, 0.625, \frac{2}{3}$, and -0.5 listed in order from least to greatest?

A. $-\frac{3}{5}, -0.5, 0.625, \frac{2}{3}$ **B.** $-0.5, -\frac{3}{5}, 0.625, \frac{2}{3}$ **C.** $-0.5, \frac{2}{3}, -\frac{3}{5}, 0.625$ **D.** $-\frac{3}{5}, \frac{2}{3}, 0.625, -0.5$

$-\frac{3}{5} = -3 \div 5 = -0.6$ ← **Write as a decimal.**

$\frac{2}{3} = 2 \div 3 = 0.66666\ldots = 0.\overline{6}$ ← **Write as a repeating decimal.**

-0.6 ▢ -0.5 ▢ 0.625 ▢ $0.\overline{6}$ ← **Compare the decimals.**

From least to greatest, the numbers are  ▢ , ▢ , ▢ , ▢ .

The correct answer is choice ▢ .

Quick Check

2. Compare -4.2 and -4.9. Use $<$, $=$, or $>$.

3. The following temperatures were recorded during a science project: $12\frac{1}{2}°$C,
$-4°$C, $6.55°$C, and $-6\frac{1}{4}°$C. Order the temperatures from least to greatest.

Lesson 1-6

Adding and Subtracting Rational Numbers

Lesson Objective	Common Core Standards
To add and subtract rational numbers	The Number System: 7.NS.1, 7.NS.1.b, 7.NS.1.c, 7.NS.1.d, 7.NS.3

Key Concepts

Distance on a Number Line

The distance between two numbers on a number line is the

[_____] .

Example

1 Adding Rational Numbers

Same Sign

The sum of two positive rational numbers is [_____] .

The sum of two negative rational numbers is [_____] .

$1\frac{1}{2} + 2\frac{1}{4}$ ← Both numbers are [_____] , so the sum is [____]

$-2.2 + (-1.5)$ ← Both numbers are [_____] , so the sum is [____]

Different Sign

Find the [_____] of each addend. Subtract the [_____]

from the [____] absolute value. The sum has the sign of the addend

with the [____] absolute value.

$-2.07 + 6.56$ ← $|-2.07| =$ [____] ; $|6.56| =$ [____]

[____] $>$ [____] , so the sum is $6.56 - 2.07 =$ [____] .

Quick Check

1. Find each sum.

  a. $-6.25 + (-8.55)$ **b.** $4\frac{3}{5} + \left(-3\frac{2}{5}\right)$ **c.** $-5.35 + 1.25$

  [_____]   [_____]   [_____]

Example

❷ **Subtracting Rational Numbers** To subtract a rational number, add its opposite.

a. Find $5\frac{5}{6} - \left(-2\frac{1}{6}\right)$.

$5\frac{5}{6} + \left(2\frac{1}{6}\right)$ ← **Add the opposite of** [ ]

So the difference is [ ]

b. Find $-1.65 - (-4.22)$.

$-1.65 + 4.22$ ← **Add the opposite of** [ ]

So the difference is [ ]

Quick Check

2. Find each difference.

a. $-3\frac{2}{5} - \left(-2\frac{4}{5}\right)$

[ ]

b. $4.35 - (-8.27)$

[ ]

c. $-13.45 - 12.25$

[ ]

Example

❸ **Application: Temperature** The temperature was $-5.5°F$ at 2:00 A.M. and $-8.0°F$ at 4:00 A.M. Find the change in temperature.

$-5.5 - (-8.0)$ ← [ ] **to find the difference.**

$-5.5 + 8.0$ ← **Add the** [ ]**.**

The difference is [ ] °F.

Quick Check

3. What is the temperature difference between $-2.5°F$ and $-6°F$?

[ ]

Lesson 1-7

Multiplying Rational Numbers

Lesson Objective	Common Core Standards
To use number lines and properties to understand multiplication of rational numbers and to multiply rational numbers	The Number System: 7.NS.2, 7.NS.2.a, 7.NS.2.c, 7.NS.3

Key Concepts

Multiplying Rational Numbers

You can use the [_____] to multiply rational numbers.

$\left(2\frac{1}{4}\right) \cdot \left(1\frac{1}{2}\right) = 2\left(1\frac{1}{2}\right) + \frac{1}{4}\left(1\frac{1}{2}\right) = \boxed{} + \boxed{} = \boxed{}$

Example

❶ **Multiplying Positive Rational Numbers** When both factors are positive, the product is positive

$3\frac{1}{3} \times 1\frac{1}{2} = \left(\boxed{} \times 1\frac{1}{2}\right)$ ← Write $3\frac{1}{3}$ as a $\boxed{}$.

$= \left(\boxed{} \times 1\frac{1}{2}\right) + \left(\boxed{} \times 1\frac{1}{2}\right)$ ← Use the Distributive Property.

$= \boxed{} + \boxed{}$ ← Multiply.

$= 5$ ← $\boxed{}$.

Quick Check

1. Find the product. Write your answer in simplest form.

   a. $4.75 \cdot 2.2$ **b.** $\left(8\frac{2}{5}\right)\left(\frac{15}{24}\right)$ **c.** $3.7 \cdot 5.1$

   [_____]   [_____]   [_____]

Example

❷ **Multiplying Negative Rational Numbers** When both factors are negative, the product is positive.

$(-2.2)(-10.4) = (-1 \cdot 2.2)(-1 \cdot 10.4)$ ← Write the negative factors as products.

$= -1 \cdot (2.2 \cdot -1) \cdot 10.4$ ← Use the $\boxed{}$ Property of Multiplication

$= -1 \cdot (-1 \cdot 2.2) \cdot 10.4$ ← Use the $\boxed{}$ Property of Multiplication

$= (-1 \cdot -1) \cdot (2.2 \cdot 10.4)$ ← Use the $\boxed{}$ Property of Multiplication

$= (1)(2.2 \cdot 10.4) = \boxed{}$ ← Multiply.

Name _____ Class _____ Date _____

Quick Check

2. Find the product. Write your answer in simplest form.

a. $\left(-2\frac{2}{3}\right)\left(-2\frac{1}{4}\right)$

b. $-7.5 \cdot (-3.1)$

c. $\left(-2\frac{2}{5}\right)\left(-1\frac{1}{3}\right)$

Example

❸ **Multiplying with Different Signs** When both factors have different signs, the product is negative.
Find $(-5.1)(1.5)$.

$(-5.1)(1.5) = (-1 \cdot 5.1)(1.5)$ ← Write the [ ] factor as a product.

$= (-1)(5.1 \cdot 1.5)$ ← Use the [ ].

$= $ [ ] ← Multiply.

Quick Check

3. Find the product. Write your answer in simplest form.

a. $\left(-\frac{3}{5}\right)\left(4\frac{1}{6}\right)$

b. $-8.5 \cdot (1.2)$

c. $\left(-1\frac{11}{16}\right)\left(\frac{8}{9}\right)$

Example

❹ **Application: Freediving** If Sofia freedives and descends $\frac{7}{8}$ ft per second below sea level, how far can she descend in 16 seconds?

$\left(-\frac{7}{8}\right)(16) = \left(-\frac{7}{8}\right)\left(\frac{16}{1}\right)$ ← Use multiplication to write an expression for the amount.

$= $ [ ] ← Multiply to find the distance below sea level.

Sofia descends [ ].

Quick Check

4. Marta is conducting a science experiment. She changes the temperature of a chemical solution by $-\frac{3}{4}$°F each minute. What is the total change in the temperature of the chemical solution after 11 minutes?

Lesson 1-8

Dividing Rational Numbers

Lesson Objective	Common Core Standards
To use the rules for dividing integers to divide rational numbers and to solve problems by dividing rational numbers	The Number System: 7.NS.2, 7.NS.2.b, 7.NS.2.c, 7.NS.3

Key Concepts

Dividing Rational Numbers

When you divide two numbers that have _____ signs, the quotient is _____.

When you divide two numbers that have _____ signs, the quotient is _____.

Example

1 Dividing Rational Numbers: Same Sign

a. Find $7.055 \div 0.85$.

$$0.85\overline{)7.055} \quad \rightarrow \quad 85\overline{)705.5}$$

Place the decimal point in the quotient above the decimal point in the dividend.

$$\begin{array}{r} 8.3 \\ 85\overline{)705.5} \\ \underline{680} \\ 255 \\ \underline{255} \\ 0 \end{array}$$

Multiply the divisor and the dividend by _____ to make the divisor a whole number.

b. Find $\left(\frac{-2}{3}\right) \div \left(\frac{-1}{2}\right)$.

$\left(-\frac{2}{3}\right) \div \left(-\frac{1}{2}\right) = \frac{-2}{3} \times \frac{-2}{1}$ ← Multiply by the _____ of the divisor.

$= (-1)\left(\frac{2}{3}\right)(-1)\left(\frac{2}{1}\right)$ ← Write −1 as a factor.

$= (-1)(-1)\left(\frac{2}{3}\right)\left(\frac{2}{1}\right)$ ← Use the _____ Property to rearrange.

$= \Box\left(\frac{2}{3}\right)\left(\frac{2}{1}\right)$ ← Multiply.

$= \Box$ or $1\frac{1}{3}$ ← Simplify if you are asked to.

Quick Check

1. Find each quotient.

a. $-16.9 \div -1.3$

b. $-\frac{2}{3} \div \frac{1}{6}$

Name _____ Class _____ Date _____

Example

❷ **Dividing Rational Numbers: Different Sign**

Find $-5\frac{1}{4} \div 2\frac{1}{2}$.

$$-5\frac{1}{4} \div 2\frac{1}{2} = \boxed{} \div \boxed{}$$ ← **Write both mixed numbers as fractions.**

$$= \left(-1 \cdot \frac{21}{4}\right) \div \frac{5}{2}$$ ← **Write the negative number as a product with −1.**

$$= \left(-1 \cdot \frac{21}{4}\right) \times \frac{2}{5}$$ ← $\boxed{}$ **by the** $\boxed{}$ **of the divisor.**

$$= (-1)\left(\frac{21}{4} \times \frac{2}{5}\right)$$ ← **Use the** $\boxed{}$ **Property.**

$$= (-1)\left(\frac{21}{10}\right)$$ ← **Multiply.**

$$= -\frac{21}{10} \text{ or } \boxed{}$$ ← **Simplify if you are asked to.**

Quick Check

2. Find each quotient.

   a. $-\frac{3}{4} \div \frac{1}{8}$

   b. $5\frac{4}{9} \div -\frac{7}{10}$

   c. $-43.68 \div 5.6$

   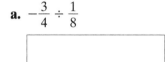

Example

❸ **Application: Paying Bills** Kendra has $159.25 left to pay on a repair bill. She will finish paying the bill in $6\frac{1}{2}$ months. How much is her monthly payment?

$$159.25 \div 6\frac{1}{2} = 159.25 \div \boxed{}$$ ← **Express both numbers as decimals.**

$$= \boxed{}$$ ← **Divide.**

Kendra will pay $\boxed{}$ each month. The last payment will be $\boxed{}$.

Check

$$6.5 \times 24.50 = \left(\boxed{} \times 24.50\right) + \left(\boxed{} \times 24.50\right)$$ ← **Use the Distributive Property.**

$$= \left(\boxed{} + \boxed{}\right).$$ ← **Multiply.**

$$= \boxed{}$$ ← **Simplify.**

Quick Check

3. Solve.

   a. Lucy owes $125.40 for repairs on her laptop. She agrees to pay this back in $5\frac{1}{2}$ weeks. By what amount will her checking account change each week to do this?

   b. Randy borrows $315.25 from his mother to buy a tablet computer. He promises to pay her back in $6\frac{1}{2}$ months. If he does this, what will his last payment be?

Lesson 2-1

Evaluating and Writing Algebraic Expressions

Lesson Objective	Common Core Standard
To write and evaluate algebraic expressions	Equations and Expressions: 7.EE.4

Vocabulary

A variable is _____

_____

An algebraic expression is _____

_____

Examples

❶ **Writing Algebraic Expressions** Write an algebraic expression for each word phrase.

a. 6 less than d dollars ☐

b. the sum of s students and 9 students ☐

c. 12 times b boxes ☐

d. 20 hours of work divided equally among w workers ☐

❷ **Art Supplies** The cost of a package of markers is d dollars. Write an algebraic expression for the total cost in dollars of 7 packages of markers.

Words | number of packages | times | cost per package |

Let d = cost per package.

Expression ☐ · ☐

An algebraic expression for the total cost in dollars is ☐ .

❸ **Writing Word Phrases** Write three different word phrases for $2y$.

_____

_____

_____

❹ Evaluating Algebraic Expressions Evaluate each expression.
Use the values $r = 8, s = 1,$ and $t = 3.$

a. $6(t - 1)$

$6(t - 1) = 6\left(\boxed{} - 1\right)$ ← **Substitute**

$\qquad = 6\left(\boxed{}\right)$ ← **Subtract.**

$\qquad = \boxed{}$ ← **Multiply.**

b. $\dfrac{r}{s + t}$

$\dfrac{r}{s + t} = \dfrac{\boxed{}}{\boxed{} + \boxed{}}$ ← **Substitute.**

$\qquad = \dfrac{\boxed{}}{\boxed{}}$ ← **Simplify the denominator.**

$\qquad = \boxed{}$ ← **Divide.**

Quick Check

1. Write an algebraic expression for a price p decreased by 16.

2. Nine students will hang t posters each. Write an algebraic expression for the total number of posters the students will hang.

3. Write three different word phrases for $c - 50$.

4. Use the values $n = 3, t = 5,$ and $y = 7$ to evaluate $(n + t) \cdot y.$

Lesson 2-2   **Simplifying Expressions**

Lesson Objective	Common Core Standard
To simplify algebraic expressions using properties of operations	Equations and Expressions: 7.EE.1

Vocabulary

Like terms are _____.

A coefficient is _____.

Examples

❶ Using Properties to Add and Subtract Simplify $6x + 10 - 4x - 12$.

$\boxed{} + 10\,\boxed{} - 12$ **Identify which parts of the expression are like terms.**

$= 6x - 4x + 10 - 12$ $\leftarrow$ $\boxed{}$ **Property of Addition**

$= (6 - 4)x + 10 - 12$ $\leftarrow$ $\boxed{}$ **Property**

$= \boxed{} + 10 - 12$ $\leftarrow$ **Simplify the coefficient.**

$= \boxed{} - \boxed{}$ $\leftarrow$ **Simplify.**

The simplified expression is $\boxed{}$.

❷ Expanding Expressions Simplify $\frac{1}{2}(6x - 8) + 11$.

$\frac{1}{2}(6x + 8) - 11$.

$= (3x + 4) - 11$ $\leftarrow$ $\boxed{}$ **Property**

$= 3x + \left(\boxed{} - 11\right)$ $\leftarrow$ **Associative Property of Addition**

$= 3x - \boxed{}$ $\leftarrow$ **Simplify**

The simplified expression is $\boxed{}$.

❸ Factoring Expressions Factor $21x + 35$.

GCF of 21 and 35 is ☐. ← **Identify the GCF.**

$21x + 35 = 7 \cdot$ ☐ $+ 7 \cdot$ ☐. ← **Factor each term by the GCF.**

$\qquad = 7\left(\text{☐} + \text{☐}\right)$ ← **Distributive Property**

The factored expression is ☐.

Quick Check

1. Simplify each expression.

a. $2x + 8 + 4x - 5$ ☐

b. $6 + 7.2y - 4.2y + 1$ ☐

c. $10r - 5 + 3 + r$ ☐

2. Simplify each expression.

a. $6(2x + 3) - 4$ ☐

b. $\frac{1}{2}(2 - 8v) + 5$ ☐

c. $9 - 4(3z + 2)$ ☐

3. Factor each expression completely.

a. $9x + 15$ ☐

b. $36 + 24t$ ☐

c. $8c - 20$ ☐

Lesson 2-3

Lesson Objective	Common Core Standard
To solve equations by adding, subtracting, multiplying, or dividing	Equations and Expressions: 7.EE.4

Vocabulary and Key Concepts

Properties of Equality

Addition Property of Equality

If you [   ] the same value to each side of an equation, the two sides remain [   ].

Subtraction Property of Equality

If you [   ] the same value from each side of an equation, the two sides remain [   ].

Division Property of Equality

If you [   ] each side of an equation by the same nonzero number, the two sides remain [   ].

Multiplication Property of Equality

If you [   ] each side of an equation by the same number, the two sides remain [   ].

Inverse operations are _____

Example

❶ Solving Equations by Adding Solve $t - 58 = 71$. Check your solution.

$t - 58 = 71$ ← [   ] **Property of Equality:**

$t - 58 + [\ ] = 71 + 58$ **Add** [ ] **to each side.**

$t + [\ ] = 129$ ← **The numbers 58 and −58 are** [   ].

$t = 129$ ← [   ] **Property**

Check [   ]   ← **Check the solution in the original equation.**

$[\ ] - 58 \stackrel{?}{=} 71$ ← **Substitute 129 for** t.

$[\ ] = 71$ ← **Subtract.**

Examples

❷ **Solving Equations by Subtracting** Your friend purchased a DVD and a CD. The DVD cost $6 more than the CD. The DVD cost $22. How much did the CD cost?

Words [   ] is $6 more than [   ].

Let c = the cost of the CD.

Equation [   ] = 6 + [   ]

$$22 = 6 + c$$
$$22 - [\quad] = 6 - [\quad] + c \quad \leftarrow \text{Subtract } [\quad] \text{ from each side.}$$
$$[\quad] = c \quad \leftarrow \text{Simplify.}$$

The CD cost [   ].

❸ **Solving Equations by Multiplying** Solve $-\frac{m}{3} = 27$.

$$-\frac{m}{3} = 27 \quad \leftarrow \text{Notice that } m \text{ is } [\quad] \text{ by } -3.$$
$$[\quad] \cdot -\frac{m}{3} = [\quad] \cdot 27 \quad \leftarrow [\quad] \text{ each side by } [\quad].$$
$$m = -81 \quad \leftarrow \text{Simplify.}$$

❹ **Solving Equations by Dividing** Solve $-3j = 44.7$.

$$-3j = 44.7 \quad \leftarrow \text{Notice } j \text{ is being } [\quad] \text{ by } -3.$$
$$\frac{-3j}{[\quad]} = \frac{44.7}{[\quad]} \quad \leftarrow [\quad] \text{ each side by } [\quad] \text{ to get } j \text{ alone.}$$
$$j = [\quad] \quad \leftarrow \text{Simplify.}$$

Quick Check

1. Solve the equation $x - 104 = 64$.

[   ]

2. A hardcover book costs $19 more than its paperback edition. The hardcover book costs $26.95. How much does the paperback cost?

[   ]

3. Solve the equation $\frac{w}{26} = -15$. Check your answer.

[   ]

4. Solve each equation. Check your answer.

a. $3x = -21.6$ [   ]

b. $-12y = -108$ [   ]

c. $104x = 312$ [   ]

Lesson 2-4

Exploring Two-Step Equations

Lesson Objective	Common Core Standard
To write and evaluate expressions with two operations and to solve two-step equations using number sense	Equations and Expressions: 7.EE.4.a

Examples

1 Writing Expressions Define a variable and write an algebraic expression for the phrase "four times the length of a rope in inches, increased by eight inches."

Let ☐ = length of rope in inches. ← **Define the variable.**

☐ · ☐ + ☐ ← **Write an algebraic expression.**

☐ + 8 ← **Rewrite 4 · ℓ as** ☐ .

2 Evaluating Expressions Evaluate the expression if the length of a rope is 9 inches.

$4\ell + 8$

4 · ☐ + 8 ← **Evaluate the expression for a rope length of** ☐ .

☐ + 8 ← **Multiply.**

☐ ← **Simplify.**

3 Using Number Sense Solve $3n - 4 = 14$ by using number sense.

$3n - 4 = 14$

■ − 4 = 14 ← **Cover 3n. Think: What number minus 4 is 14?**
         Answer: ☐ .

$3n =$ ☐ ← **So** ■ **, or 3n, must equal** ☐ .

3 · ■ = ☐ ← **Now cover n. Think: What number times 3 is** ☐ **?**
         Answer: ☐

$n =$ ☐ ← **So** ■ **, or n, must equal** ☐ .

Check

$3n - 4 = 14$ ← **Check your solution in the original equation.**

$3(6) - 4 \stackrel{?}{=} 14$ ← **Substitute 6 for n.**

$18 - 4 \stackrel{?}{=} 14$ ← **Simplify.**

$14 = 14$ ← **The solution checks.**

④ Shopping The Healy family wants to buy a TV that costs $200. They already have $80 saved toward the cost. How much will they have to save per month for the next six months in order to have the whole cost saved?

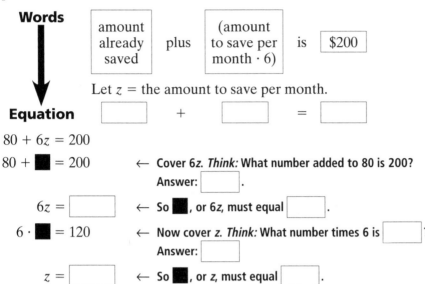

Words

| amount already saved | plus | (amount to save per month · 6) | is | $200 |

Let z = the amount to save per month.

Equation [ ] + [ ] = [ ]

$80 + 6z = 200$

$80 + \blacksquare = 200$ ← **Cover 6z. Think: What number added to 80 is 200?**
　　　　　　　　　　　Answer: [ ] .

$6z = $ [ ] ← **So** $\blacksquare$ **, or 6z, must equal** [ ] .

$6 \cdot \blacksquare = 120$ ← **Now cover z. Think: What number times 6 is** [ ] **?**
　　　　　　　　　　　Answer: [ ] .

$z = $ [ ] ← **So** $\blacksquare$ **, or z, must equal** [ ] .

They will have to save [ ] per month.

Quick Check

1. Define a variable and write an algebraic expression for "a man is two years younger than three times his son's age."

[   ]

2. Evaluate the expression to find the man's age if his son is 13.

[   ]

3. Solve each equation using number sense.

　a. $3m + 9 = 21$ [   ]

　b. $8d + 5 = 45$ [   ]

　c. $4y - 11 = 33$ [   ]

4. Basketball During the first half of a game you scored 8 points. In the second half you made only 3-point baskets. You finished the game with 23 points. Write and solve an equation to find how many 3-point baskets you made.

[   ]

Lesson 2-5

Solving Two-Step Equations

Lesson Objective	Common Core Standards
To solve two-step equations using inverse operations	Equations and Expressions: 7.EE.3, 7.EE.4.a

Examples

❶ Undoing Subtraction First Solve $6r - 19 = 41$.

$$6r - 19 = 41$$

$6r - 19 + \boxed{} = 41 + \boxed{}$ ← To undo $\boxed{}$, add $\boxed{}$ to each side.

$6r = 60$ ← Simplify.

$\dfrac{6r}{\boxed{}} = \dfrac{60}{\boxed{}}$ ← To undo $\boxed{}$, divide each side by $\boxed{}$.

$r = \boxed{}$ ← Simplify.

Check $6r - 19 = 41$ ← Check your solution in the original equation.

$6\left(\boxed{}\right) - 19 \stackrel{?}{=} 41$ ← Substitute $\boxed{}$ for r.

$\boxed{} - 19 \stackrel{?}{=} 41$ ← Simplify.

$\boxed{} = 41$ ✓ ← The solution checks.

❷ Undoing Addition First Solve $\frac{a}{5} + 4 = 10$.

$$\frac{a}{5} + 4 = 10$$

$\frac{a}{5} + 4 \boxed{} 4 = 10 \boxed{} 4$ ← To undo addition, $\boxed{}$ 4 from each side.

$\frac{a}{5} = 6$ ← Simplify.

$\left(\boxed{}\right)\left(\frac{a}{5}\right) = \left(\boxed{}\right)(6)$ ← To undo division, multiply each side by $\boxed{}$.

$a = \boxed{}$ ← Simplify.

❸ Solving Two-Step Equations An amusement park charges $15.00 for admission and $.50 for each ride. You spend $27.00 total. How many rides did you go on?

A. 54   **B.** 43   **C.** 24   **D.** 6

Words   [ ] times [the number of rides] plus [ ] is 27.

Let n = number of rides you went on.

Equation   [ ] · n +   [ ] = 27

[ ] · n + [ ] = 27

[ ] · n + [ ] − 15 = 27 − 15   ← **Subtract 15 from each side.**

[ ] · n = 12   ← **Simplify.**

$$\frac{0.50n}{0.50} = \frac{12}{0.50}$$ ← **Divide each side by** [ ].

n = [ ]   ← **Simplify.**

You went on [ ] rides. The correct answer is choice [ ].

Quick Check

1. Solve the equation $-8y - 28 = -36$. Check your answer.

2. Solve the equation $\frac{x}{5} + 35 = 75$. Check your answer.

3. Solomon decides to make posters for the student council election. He bought markers that cost $.79 each and a poster board that cost $1.25. The total cost was $7.57. Write and solve an equation to find the number of markers that Solomon bought.

Lesson 2-6

Solving Equations Involving the Distributive Property

Lesson Objective	Common Core Standards
To solve equations of the form $p(x + q) = r$ using the Distributive Property	Equations and Expressions: 7.EE.3, 7.EE.4.a

Key Concepts

Distributive Property

When you multiply a factor by a sum (or difference), the product is the same as multiplying the factor by each term and then adding (or subtracting) the products.

Arithmetic	Algebra
$4(5 + 9) = 4(5) + 4(9)$ $4(14) = 20 + 36$ $56 = 56$	$p(x + q) = px + pq$

Examples

❶ Using the Distributive Property Let $x =$ the length of a rectangular card. If the width of the card is 3.5 inches, and the perimeter is 17 inches, what is the length of the card?

Solve $2(x + 3.5) = 17$.

$2(x + 3.5) = 17$ ← **Write the equation for perimeter**

$2x + 2(3.5) = 17$ ← **Use the** ⬚ **Property**

$2x + 7 = 17$ ← **Simplify**

$2x = 10$ ← **Subtract** ⬚ **from both sides**

⬚ = ⬚   ← **Divide both sides by 2.**

The length of the card is ⬚ .

❷ Solve using the Distributive Property Solve $4(d - 1.5) = -8$.

$$4(d - 1.5) = -8$$

$$4\boxed{} - 4\left(\boxed{}\right) = -8 \qquad \leftarrow \textbf{Use the Distributive Property}$$

$$4x - 6 = -8 \qquad \leftarrow \textbf{Simplify each side.}$$

$$4x = \boxed{} \qquad \leftarrow \textbf{Add 6 to both sides}$$

$$\boxed{} = \boxed{} \qquad \leftarrow \textbf{Divide both sides by 2.}$$

Check $4(-0.5) - 4(1.5) = -2 - 6$

$$= -8$$

The solution checks.

Quick Check

1. What is the width of a rectangle with a length of 17 centimeters and a perimeter of 58 centimeters?

2. Solve these equations.

a. $-4.5 = -3(b + 15)$

b. $8\frac{1}{2}(c - 16) = 340$

Lesson 3-1

Graphing and Writing Inequalities

Lesson Objective	Common Core Standard
To graph and write algebraic inequalities	Equations and Expressions: 7.EE.4.b

Vocabulary

An inequality is _____

_____

A solution of an inequality is _____

_____

Examples

❶ Identifying Solutions of an Inequality Find whether each number is a solution of $k > -6$; $-8, -6, 0, 3, 7$.

Test each value by replacing the variable and evaluating the sentence.

$-8 > -6$ ← −8 is greater than −6; false.

$-6 > -6$ ← −6 is greater than −6; [____].

$0 > -6$ ← 0 is greater than −6; [____].

$3 > -6$ ← 3 is [____] than −6; [____].

$7 > -6$ ← 7 is [____] than −6; [____].

The numbers [____], [____], and [____] are solutions of $k > -6$.

The numbers [____] and [____] are not solutions of $k > -6$.

❷ Graphing Inequalities Graph the solution of each inequality on a number line.

a. $r \leq 2$

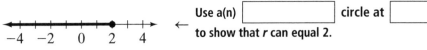

← Use a(n) [_____] circle at [____]
to show that r can equal 2.

b. $m > -5$

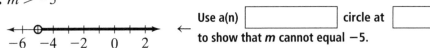

← Use a(n) [_____] circle at [____]
to show that m cannot equal −5.

Name _____ Class _____ Date _____

❸ Writing Inequalities Write an inequality for the graph.

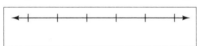

← Since the circle at 1 is closed,

Since the circle at 1 is closed,

1 [   ] a solution.

y [ ] 1   ← Since the graph shows values [   ] or [   ] 1, use [ ].

❹ Social Studies You must be at least 18 years of age to vote in a presidential election in the United States. Write an inequality for this requirement.

Words   [   ] is [   ] [   ]

⬇

Let [a] = age in years.

Inequality   [ ]   [ ]   [ ]

The inequality is [   ].

Quick Check

1. Which numbers are solutions of the inequality $m \geq -3; -8, -2, 1.4$?

[   ]

2. Graph the solution of the inequality $w < -3$.

[⟵+——+——+——+——+——+——+——+——+⟶]

3. Write an inequality for the graph.

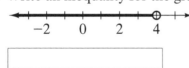

[   ]

4. Write an inequality for "To qualify for the race, your time can be at most 62 seconds."

[   ]

Name _____ Class _____ Date _____

Lesson 3-2

Solving Inequalities by Adding or Subtracting

Lesson Objective	Common Core Standard
To solve inequalities by adding or subtracting	Equations and Expressions: 7.EE.4.b

Key Concepts

Addition Property of Inequality

You can [   ] the same value to each side of an inequality.

Arithmetic

Since $7 > 3, 7 + 4 > 3 +$ [ ].

Since $1 < 3, 1 +$ [ ] $< 3 + 4$.

Algebra

If $a > b$, then $a +$ [ ] $> b + c$.

If $a < b$, then $a + c < b +$ [ ].

Subtraction Property of Inequality

You can [   ] the same value from each side of an inequality.

Arithmetic

Since $9 > 6, 9 - 3 > 6 -$ [ ].

Since $15 < 20, 15 -$ [ ] $< 20 - 4$.

Algebra

If $a > b$, then $a -$ [ ] $> b - c$.

If $a < b$, then $a - c < b -$ [ ].

Examples

❶ Solving Inequalities by Adding Solve $q - 2 \geq -6$. Graph the solution.

$$q - 2 \geq -6$$
$$q - 2 + \boxed{} \geq -6 + \boxed{} \qquad \leftarrow \text{ Add } \boxed{} \text{ to each side.}$$
$$q \geq \boxed{} \qquad \leftarrow \text{ Simplify.}$$

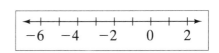

❷ Solving Inequalities by Subtracting Solve $d + 9 < 8$.
Graph the solution.

$$d + 9 < 8$$
$$d + 9 - \boxed{} < 8 - \boxed{} \qquad \leftarrow \text{ Subtract } \boxed{} \text{ from each side.}$$
$$q < \boxed{} \qquad \leftarrow \text{ Simplify.}$$

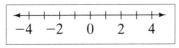

Example

❸ **Budget** The Drama Club can spend no more than $120 for costumes. They already spent $79. How much more can they spend for costumes?

Words
⬇

| amount spent already | plus | amount spent on costumes | is at most | $120. |

Let c = amount the Drama Club can spend on costumes.

Inequality $\boxed{}$ $+$ $\boxed{}$ $\boxed{}$ $\boxed{}$

$$79 + c \leq 120$$

$79 - \boxed{} + c \leq 120 - \boxed{}$ ← **Subtract** $\boxed{}$ **from each side.**

$c \leq \boxed{}$ ← **Simplify.**

They can spend at most $\boxed{}$.

Quick Check

1. Solve $y - 3 < 4$. Graph the solution.

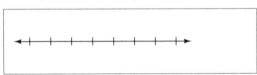

2. Solve each inequality. Graph the solution.

a. $x + 9 > 5$

b. $y + 3 < 4$

c. $w + 4 \leq -5$

3. To get an A, you need more than 200 points on a two-part test. You score 109 points on the first part. How many more points do you need?

Lesson 3-3

Solving Inequalities by Multiplying or Dividing

Lesson Objective	Common Core Standard
To solve inequalities by multiplying or dividing	Equations and Expressions: 7.EE.4.b

Key Concepts

Division Property of Inequality

If you [ ] each side of an inequality by the same positive number, the direction of the inequality symbol remains unchanged.

Arithmetic

$9 > 6$, so $\dfrac{9}{3}$ [ ] $\dfrac{6}{3}$

$15 < 20$, so $\dfrac{15}{5}$ [ ] $\dfrac{\boxed{}}{\boxed{}}$

Algebra

If $a > b$, and c is positive, then $\dfrac{a}{c}$ [ ] $\dfrac{b}{c}$.

If $a < b$, and c is positive, then $\dfrac{a}{c}$ [ ] $\dfrac{\boxed{}}{\boxed{}}$.

If you [ ] each side of an inequality by the same negative number, the direction of the inequality symbol is reversed.

Arithmetic

$16 > 12$, so $-\dfrac{16}{4}$ [ ] $-\dfrac{12}{4}$

$10 < 18$, so $-\dfrac{10}{2}$ [ ] $\dfrac{\boxed{}}{\boxed{}}$

Algebra

If $a > b$, and c is negative, then $\dfrac{a}{c}$ [ ] $\dfrac{b}{c}$.

If $a < b$, and c is negative, then $\dfrac{a}{c}$ [ ] $\dfrac{\boxed{}}{\boxed{}}$.

Multiplication Property of Inequality

If you [ ] each side of an inequality by the same positive number, the direction of the inequality symbol remains unchanged.

Arithmetic

$12 > 8$, so $12 \cdot 2$ [ ] [ ] $\cdot 2$

$3 < 6$, so $3 \cdot 4$ [ ] [ ] $\cdot 4$

Algebra

If $a > b$, and c is positive, then $a \cdot c$ [ ] [ ] $\cdot c$.

If $a < b$, and c is positive, then $a \cdot c$ [ ] [ ] $\cdot c$.

If you [ ] each side of an inequality by the same negative number, the direction of the inequality symbol is reversed.

Arithmetic

$6 > 2$, so $6(-3)$ [ ] [ ] (-3)

$3 < 5$, so $3(-2)$ [ ] [ ] (-2)

Algebra

If $a > b$, and c is negative, then $a \cdot c$ [ ] [ ] $\cdot c$.

If $a < b$, and c is negative, then $a \cdot c$ [ ] [ ] $\cdot c$.

Name _____ Class _____ Date _____

Examples

 Business A woodworker makes a profit of $30 on each picture frame that is sold. Write an inequality to describe the number of frames the woodworker must sell to make a profit of at least $500.

Words → | number of frames | times | profit on each frame | is at least | $500 |

Let f = the number of frames.

Inequality ☐ · ☐ ☐ ☐

$30f \geq 500$

$\dfrac{30f}{30} \geq \dfrac{500}{30}$ ← **Divide each side by 30.**

$f \geq 16.\overline{6}$ ← **Simplify.**

$f \geq 17$ ← **Round up to the nearest whole number.**

The woodworker must sell at least ☐ frames.

② **Solving Inequalities by Multiplying** Solve $\dfrac{b}{-3} < -12$.

$$\dfrac{b}{-3} < -12$$

☐ · $-\dfrac{b}{3}$ ☐ ☐ · -12 ← **Multiply each side by ☐.**
                                    Reverse the direction of the symbol.

b ☐ ☐   ← **Simplify.**

Quick Check

1. A long-distance telephone company is offering a special rate of $.06 per minute. Your budget for long-distance telephone calls is $25 for the month. At most how many minutes of long distance can you use for the month?

2. Solve $-\dfrac{k}{5} < -4$. Graph the solution.

Lesson 3-4

Solving Two-Step Inequalities

Lesson Objective	Common Core Standard
To solve two-step inequalities using inverse operations	Equations and Expressions: 7.EE.4.b

Examples

❶ Undoing Subtraction First Solve $\frac{n}{3} - 5 \geq -4$. Graph the solution.

$$\frac{n}{3} - 5 \geq -4$$

$$\frac{n}{3} - 5 + \boxed{} \geq -4 + \boxed{} \qquad \leftarrow \text{ Add } \boxed{} \text{ to each side.}$$

$$\frac{n}{3} \geq \boxed{} \qquad \leftarrow \text{ Simplify.}$$

$$\boxed{} \cdot \frac{n}{3} \geq \boxed{} \cdot 1 \qquad \leftarrow \text{ Multiply each side by } \boxed{}.$$

$$n \geq \boxed{} \qquad \leftarrow \text{ Simplify.}$$

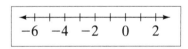

❷ Undoing Addition First Solve $-4.4x + 2 > 8.6$. Graph the solution.

$$-4.4x + 2 > 8.6$$

$$-4.4x + 2 - \boxed{} > 8.6 - \boxed{} \qquad \leftarrow \text{ Subtract } \boxed{} \text{ from each side.}$$

$$\boxed{} > 6.6 \qquad \leftarrow \text{ Simplify.}$$

$$\frac{-4.4x}{\boxed{}} < \frac{6.6}{\boxed{}} \qquad \leftarrow \text{ Divide each side by } -4.4.$$

$$x < \boxed{} \qquad \leftarrow \text{ Simplify.}$$

❸ **Archery** An archery range charges $50 for membership plus $5 per round. Vivian wants to join the range and shoot as many rounds as possible, but she has only $75. What is the greatest number of rounds she can shoot?

Words

| cost per round | times | number of rounds | plus | membership fee | is at most | total cost |

Let r = the number of rounds

Expression

$\boxed{}$ · $\boxed{}$ + $\boxed{}$ = $\boxed{}$

$5r + 50 \leq 75$

$5r + 50 - 50 \leq 75 - 50$ ← **Subtract** $\boxed{}$ from each side.

$5r \leq \boxed{}$ ← **Simplify.**

$\dfrac{5r}{\boxed{}} \leq \dfrac{25}{\boxed{}}$ ← **Divide each side by** $\boxed{}$.

$r \leq \boxed{}$ ← **Simplify.**

Quick Check

1. Solve the inequality $-5 + \frac{c}{3} > -1$. Graph the solution.

2. Solve $\frac{1}{5} \geq -\frac{1}{3a} + \frac{1}{2}$. Graph the solution on a number line.

3. A phone plan charges $.20 per text message plus a monthly fee of $42.50. Lin can spend at most $50. Write an inequality for the number of text messages Lin can send. Describe the solution.

Lesson 4-1

Ratios

Lesson Objective

To write ratios and use them to compare quantities

Vocabulary and Key Concepts

Ratio

A ratio is _____

You can write a ratio in three ways.

Arithmetic				**Algebra**	

5 to 7   [   ]   ⬚/⬚   [   ] $a : b$ $\dfrac{\square}{\square}$, where $b \neq 0$

Equivalent ratios are _____

Example

1 Writing Ratios There are 7 red stripes and 6 white stripes on the flag of the United States. Write the ratio of red stripes to white stripes in three ways.

red stripes → [   ] ← white stripes

red stripes → [   ] ← white stripes

⬚ ← red stripes

⬚ ← white stripes

Quick Check

1. Write each ratio in three ways. Use the pattern of piano keys shown at the right.

   a. white keys to all keys

   b. white keys to black keys

Examples

❷ **Writing Equivalent Ratios** Find a ratio equivalent to $\frac{14}{4}$.

$$\frac{14 \div \boxed{}}{4 \div \boxed{}} = \frac{\boxed{}}{\boxed{}} \qquad \leftarrow \text{Divide the numerator and denominator by 2.}$$

❸ **Writing Equivalent Ratios** Write the ratio 2 lb to 56 oz as a fraction in simplest form.

$$\frac{2 \text{ lb}}{56 \text{ oz}} = \frac{2 \times 16 \text{ oz}}{56 \text{ oz}} \qquad \leftarrow \text{There are 16 oz in each pound.}$$

$$= \frac{\boxed{} \text{ oz}}{56 \text{ oz}} \qquad \leftarrow \text{Multiply.}$$

$$= \frac{\boxed{} \div \boxed{} \text{ oz}}{56 \div \boxed{} \text{ oz}} \qquad \leftarrow \text{Divide by the GCF, } \boxed{} \text{ oz.}$$

$$= \frac{\boxed{}}{\boxed{}} \qquad \leftarrow \text{Simplify.}$$

❹ **Comparing Ratios** The ratio of girls to boys enrolled at King Middle School is 15 : 16. There are 195 girls and 208 boys in Grade 8. Is the ratio of girls to boys in Grade 8 equivalent to the ratio of girls to boys in the entire school?

Entire School				**Grade 8**
$\boxed{}$	$\leftarrow$	girls	$\rightarrow$	$\boxed{}$
$\boxed{}$	$\leftarrow$	boys	$\rightarrow$	$\boxed{}$

$$\frac{\boxed{}}{\boxed{}} = \boxed{} \quad \leftarrow \text{Write as a decimal.} \rightarrow \quad \frac{\boxed{}}{\boxed{}} = \boxed{}$$

Since the two decimals are $\boxed{}$, the ratio of girls to boys in Grade 8 is $\boxed{}$ to the ratio of girls to boys in the entire school.

Quick Check

2. Find a ratio equivalent to $\frac{7}{9}$.

$\boxed{}$

3. Write the ratio 3 gal to 10 qt as a fraction in simplest form.

$\boxed{}$

4. Tell whether the ratios below are *equivalent* or *not equivalent*.

a. $7 : 3, 128 : 54$

$\boxed{}$

b. $\frac{180}{240}, \frac{25}{34}$

$\boxed{}$

c. 6.1 to 7, 30.5 to 35

$\boxed{}$

Lesson 4-2   Unit Rates and Proportional Reasoning

Lesson Objective	Common Core Standard
To find unit rates and unit costs using proportional reasoning	Ratios and Proportional Relationships: 7.RP.1

Vocabulary

A rate is _____

_____

A unit rate is _____

A unit cost is _____

Examples

❶ **Finding a Unit Rate Using Whole Numbers** You earn $33 for 4 hours of work. Find the unit rate of dollars per hour.

dollars → $\dfrac{33}{4}$ = [   ]   ← **Divide the first quantity by**
hours →   **the second quantity.**

The unit rate is $\dfrac{\boxed{}}{\boxed{}}$, or [   ] per hour.

❷ **Finding a Unit Rate Using Fractions** Ely walks $\frac{7}{8}$ mile in $\frac{1}{3}$ hour. What is his speed in miles per hour?

miles to hours $= \dfrac{7}{8}$ to $\dfrac{1}{3}$ →   **Write the ratio.**

miles [ ] hours $= \dfrac{7}{8} \div \dfrac{\boxed{}}{\boxed{}}$ →   **Divide the first quantity by the second quantity.**

$= \dfrac{\boxed{}}{\boxed{}}$ →   **Simplify.**

$= \boxed{}\,\dfrac{\boxed{}}{\boxed{}}$ →   **Write as a mixed number.**

Ely walks $\boxed{}\,\dfrac{\boxed{}}{\boxed{}}$ miles [ ] [ ].

Quick Check

1. Find the unit rate for 210 heartbeats in 3 minutes.

2. Find the unit rate for $\frac{3}{10}$ mile in $\frac{3}{4}$ hour.

Example

❸ Using Unit Cost to Compare Find each unit cost. Which is the better buy?

3 lb of potatoes for $.89
5 lb of potatoes for $1.59

Divide to find the unit cost of each size.

cost → $\frac{\$.89}{3\ lb}$ ≈ ⬚

cost → $\frac{\$1.59}{5\ lb}$ ≈ ⬚

Since ⬚ < ⬚ , ⬚ for ⬚

is the better buy.

Quick Check

3. Which bottle of apple juice is the better buy: 48 fl oz of fruit juice for $3.05 or 64 fl oz for $3.59?

Lesson 4-3
Proportions

Lesson Objective	Common Core Standards
To test whether ratios form a proportion by using equivalent ratios and cross products	Ratios and Proportional Relationships: 7.RP.2, 7.RP.2.a

Key Concepts

Proportion

A proportion is _____

Arithmetic	**Algebra**
$\frac{1}{2} = \frac{2}{4}$	$\frac{a}{b} = \frac{c}{d}, b \neq 0, d \neq 0$

Cross Products Property

Cross products are _____

_____

If two ratios form a proportion, the cross products are equal. If two ratios have equal cross products, they form a proportion.

Arithmetic	**Algebra**
$\frac{6}{8} = \frac{9}{12}$	$\frac{a}{b} = \frac{c}{d}$
$6 \cdot 12 = 8 \cdot 9$	$ad = bc$, where $b \neq 0$, and $d \neq 0$

Example

1 Writing Ratios in Simplest Form Do the ratios $\frac{42}{56}$ and $\frac{56}{64}$ form a proportion?

$\frac{42}{56} = \frac{42 \div \boxed{}}{56 \div \boxed{}} = \frac{\boxed{}}{\boxed{}}$ ← **Divide the numerator and denominator by the GCF.** → $\frac{56}{64} = \frac{56 \div \boxed{}}{64 \div \boxed{}} = \frac{\boxed{}}{\boxed{}}$

The ratios in simplest form are not equivalent. They $\boxed{}$ form a proportion.

Quick Check

1. Do $\frac{10}{12}$ and $\frac{40}{56}$ form a proportion?

$\boxed{}$

Example

② Using Cross Products Do the ratios in each pair form a proportion?

a. $\frac{4}{10}, \frac{6}{15}$ **b.** $\frac{8}{6}, \frac{9}{7}$

$$\frac{4}{10} \stackrel{?}{=} \frac{6}{15} \qquad \leftarrow \text{ Test each pair of ratios. } \rightarrow \qquad \frac{8}{6} \stackrel{?}{=} \frac{9}{7}$$

$$4 \cdot \boxed{} \stackrel{?}{=} 10 \cdot \boxed{} \qquad \leftarrow \text{ Write cross products. } \rightarrow \quad 8 \cdot \boxed{} \stackrel{?}{=} 6 \cdot \boxed{}$$

$$\boxed{}\boxed{} 60 \qquad \leftarrow \text{ Simplify. } \rightarrow \qquad \boxed{}\boxed{} 54$$

$$\boxed{}, \frac{4}{10} \text{ and } \frac{6}{15} \qquad\qquad\qquad \boxed{}, \frac{8}{6} \text{ and } \frac{9}{7}$$

$\boxed{}$ a proportion. $\boxed{}$ a proportion.

Quick Check

2. Determine whether the ratios form a proportion.

a. $\frac{3}{8}, \frac{6}{16}$ **b.** $\frac{6}{9}, \frac{4}{6}$ **c.** $\frac{4}{8}, \frac{5}{9}$

Lesson 4-4

Solving Proportions

Lesson Objective	Common Core Standards
To solve proportions using unit rates, mental math, and cross products	Ratios and Proportional Relationships: 7.RP.1, 7.RP.2

Examples

❶ Using Unit Rates The cost of 4 lightbulbs is $3. Use the information to find the cost of 10 lightbulbs.

Step 1 Find the unit price.

$$\frac{3 \text{ dollars}}{4 \text{ lightbulbs}} = \$3 \div 4 \text{ lightbulbs} \quad \leftarrow \textbf{Divide to find the unit price.}$$

$$\frac{\boxed{}}{\text{lightbulb}}$$

Step 2 You know the cost of one lightbulb. Multiply to find the cost of 10 lightbulbs.

$$\boxed{} \cdot \boxed{} = \boxed{} \quad \leftarrow \textbf{Multiply the unit rate by the number of lightbulbs.}$$

The cost of 10 lightbulbs is $\boxed{}$.

❷ Solving Using Mental Math Solve each proportion using mental math.

a. $\frac{5}{c} = \frac{30}{42}$

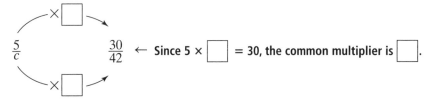

$\leftarrow$ Since $5 \times \boxed{} = 30$, the common multiplier is $\boxed{}$.

$c = \boxed{}$ $\leftarrow$ Use mental math to find what number times $\boxed{}$ equals 42.

b. $\frac{9}{4} = \frac{72}{t}$

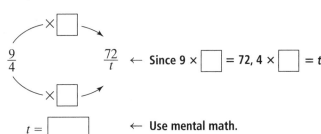

$\leftarrow$ Since $9 \times \boxed{} = 72$, $4 \times \boxed{} = t$.

$t = \boxed{}$ $\leftarrow$ Use mental math.

❸ **Solving Using Cross Products** Solve $\frac{6}{8} = \frac{9}{a}$ using cross products.

$$\frac{6}{8} = \frac{9}{a}$$

$6a = 8(9)$ ← **Write the cross products.**

$6a = \boxed{}$ ← **Simplify.**

$\dfrac{6a}{\boxed{}} = \dfrac{\boxed{}}{\boxed{}}$ ← **Divide each side by** $\boxed{}$.

$a = \boxed{}$ ← **Simplify.**

Quick Check

1. **a.** Postcards cost $2.45 for 5 cards. How much will 13 cards cost?

   [ ]

   b. Swimming goggles cost $84.36 for 12. At this rate, how much will new goggles for 17 members of a swim team cost?

   [ ]

2. Solve each proportion using mental math.

   a. $\dfrac{3}{8} = \dfrac{b}{24}$

   [ ]

   b. $\dfrac{m}{5} = \dfrac{16}{40}$

   [ ]

   c. $\dfrac{15}{30} = \dfrac{5}{p}$

   [ ]

3. Solve each proportion using cross products.

   a. $\dfrac{12}{15} = \dfrac{x}{21}$

   [ ]

   b. $\dfrac{16}{30} = \dfrac{d}{51}$

   [ ]

   c. $\dfrac{20}{35} = \dfrac{110}{m}$

   [ ]

Lesson 4-5

Similar Figures

Lesson Objective	Common Core Standards
To use proportions to find missing lengths in similar figures	Ratios and Proportional Relationships: 7.RP.1, 7.RP.2, 7.G.1

Vocabulary and Key Concepts

Similar Polygons

Two polygons are similar if

- corresponding angles _____
- the lengths of corresponding sides _____

A polygon is _____

_____

Indirect measurement is _____

_____

Example

① **Finding a Missing Measure** $\triangle ABC$ and $\triangle DEF$ are similar. Find the value of c.

$$\frac{AB}{DE} = \frac{AC}{DF}$$ ← **Write a proportion.**

$$\frac{c}{\boxed{}} = \frac{6}{\boxed{}}$$ ← **Substitute.**

$$\frac{c}{\boxed{}} = \frac{2}{\boxed{}}$$ ← **Write** $\frac{6}{\boxed{}}$ **in simplest form.**

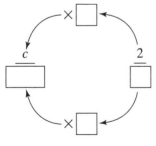 ← **Find the common multiplier.**

$c = \boxed{}$ ← **Use mental math.**

Name _____ Class _____ Date _____

❷ Multiple Choice A 5-ft person standing near a tree has a shadow
12 ft long. At the same time, the tree has a shadow 42 ft long. What is the
height of the tree?

A. 17.5 ft   **B.** 35 ft   **C.** 49 ft   **D.** 100.8 ft

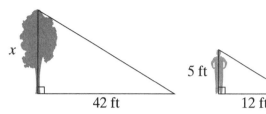

Draw a picture and let x represent the height of the tree.

$\dfrac{x}{\boxed{}} = \dfrac{42}{\boxed{}}$ ← **Write a proportion.**

$\boxed{} \, x = \boxed{} \cdot 42$ ← **Write the cross products.**

$\dfrac{12x}{12} = \dfrac{5 \cdot 42}{12}$ ← **Divide each side by 12.**

$x = \boxed{}$ ← **Simplify.**

The height of the tree is $\boxed{}$ ft. The correct answer is choice $\boxed{}$.

Quick Check

1. The trapezoids below are similar. Find x.

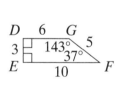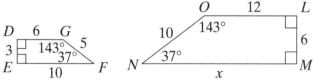

2. A 6-ft person has a shadow 5 ft long. A nearby tree has a shadow 30 ft long.
What is the height of the tree?

Lesson 4-6

Maps and Scale Drawings

Lesson Objective	Common Core Standards
To use proportions to solve problems involving scale	Ratios and Proportional Relationships: 7.G.1, 7.RP.1

Vocabulary

A scale drawing is _____

_____

A scale is _____

_____

Example

❶ **Using a Scale Drawing** The scale of a drawing is 1 in. : 6 ft. The length of a wall is 4.5 in. on the drawing. Find the actual length of the wall.

You can write the scale of the drawing as $\frac{1 \text{ in.}}{6 \text{ ft}}$. Then write a proportion.

Let n represent the actual length.

drawing (in.) → $\dfrac{1}{6} = \dfrac{\boxed{}}{n}$ ← drawing (in.)
actual (ft) → $\phantom{\dfrac{1}{6}}$ ← actual (ft)

$\boxed{} n = \boxed{} (4.5)$ ← Write the cross products.

$n = \boxed{}$ ← Simplify.

The actual length is $\boxed{}$ ft.

Quick Check

1. The chimney of a house is 4 cm tall on the drawing. How tall is the chimney of the actual house?

1 cm = 2.5 m

Examples

❷ **Finding the Scale of a Model** The actual length of the wheelbase of a mountain bike is 260 cm. The length of the wheelbase in a scale drawing is 4 cm. Find the scale of the drawing.

scale length → $\dfrac{4}{260} = \dfrac{4 \div \boxed{}}{260 \div \boxed{}} = \dfrac{\boxed{}}{\boxed{}}$ ← **Write the ratio in simplest form.**
actual length →

The scale is $\boxed{}$ cm : $\boxed{}$ cm.

❸ **Multiple Choice** You want to make a scale model of a house that is 72 feet long and 24 feet tall. You plan to make the model 12 inches long. Which equation can you use to find x, the height of the model?

A. $\dfrac{24}{72} = \dfrac{x}{12}$ **B.** $\dfrac{12}{72} = \dfrac{x}{24}$ **C.** $\dfrac{12}{24} = \dfrac{x}{72}$ **D.** $\dfrac{x}{24} = \dfrac{72}{12}$

model (in.) → $\dfrac{\boxed{}}{\boxed{}} = \dfrac{\boxed{?}}{\boxed{?}}$ ← **model (in.)**
actual (ft) →   ← **actual (ft)**   ← **Write a proportion.**

$\dfrac{\boxed{}}{\boxed{}} = \dfrac{\boxed{}}{\boxed{}}$ ← **Fill in the information you know. Use x for the information you don't know.**

The correct answer is $\boxed{}$.

Quick Check

2. The length of a room in an architectural drawing is 10 in. Its actual length is 160 in. What is the scale of the drawing?

$\boxed{}$

3. You want to make a scale model of a sailboat that is 51 ft long and 15 ft wide. You plan to make the sailboat 17 in. long. How wide should the model be?

$\boxed{}$

Lesson 4-7

Proportional Relationships

Lesson Objective	Common Core Standards
To identify proportional relationships and find constants of proportionality	Ratios and Proportions: 7.RP.2.a, 7.RP.2.b, 7.RP.2.c, 7.RP.2.d

Vocabulary

A constant of proportionality is _____

_____

Examples

❶ Using a Table to Determine a Proportional Relationship The table below
shows the number of times Linda skipped rope in minutes during a fundraiser.
Is there a proportional relationship between time and skips?

Compare the ratios of time and rope skips.

Minutes	0	5	12	15	17
Skips	0	150	360	450	510

$$\text{rope skips} \rightarrow \frac{150}{5} = \frac{\boxed{}}{12} = \frac{450}{\boxed{}} = \frac{\boxed{}}{\boxed{}}$$
time →

The ratios are $\boxed{}$, so there is a $\boxed{}$ relationship
between time and $\boxed{}$.

❷ Using a Graph to Find a Unit Rate The graph below displays the data given in Example 1.
What is Linda's speed in skips per minute?

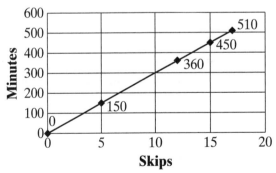

Linda's speed is a unit rate. Find the value of r in the ordered pair $(1, r)$.

The graph of this relationship passes through $(0, 0)$ and $\left(\boxed{}, 150\right)$. So, it must also

pass through $\left(1, \boxed{}\right)$. Since $r = \boxed{}$, the unit rate is $\boxed{}\ \boxed{}$ per $\boxed{}$.

Linda's speed is $\boxed{}\ \boxed{}$ per $\boxed{}$.

Name _____ Class _____ Date _____

❸ Using a Ratio to Identify a Unit Rate The table below shows a proportional relationship between the number of songs downloaded on a music site and the amount the customer pays. Identify the constant of proportionality.

Step 1 Use one data point to find the constant of proportionality c.

Songs Downloaded, s	Price, p (dollars)
20	$10
40	$20
100	$50
120	$60

$\dfrac{\text{price}}{\text{songs}} = \dfrac{\boxed{}}{\boxed{}}$ ← **Find the price per song by** $\boxed{}$ **the** $\boxed{}$ **by the number of** $\boxed{}$.

$= \boxed{}$ ← **Simplify.**

Step 2 Check by multiplying c times the first quantity.

$20 \times \boxed{} = \boxed{}$ $40 \times \boxed{} = \boxed{}$

$100 \times \boxed{} = \boxed{}$ $120 \times \boxed{} = \boxed{}$

The constant of proportionality is $\boxed{}$. This unit rate represents a payment of $\boxed{}$ per song.

Quick Check

1. The table at the right shows the distances Dave rode in a bike-a-thon. Is there a proportional relationship? Explain.

_____

_____

Dave

Hours	0	3	6	8	9
Miles	0	18.6	35.2	49.6	56.8

2. Use the graph at the right. What is Damon's reading speed in pages per day?

_____

_____

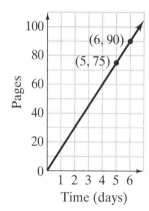

3. Find the constant of proportionality for each table of values.

a. yards of cloth per blanket

Yards(y)	16	32	40
Blankets (b)	8	16	20

b. pay per hour

Hours(h)	2	10	16
Pay (p)	$11	$55	$88

_____   _____

Lesson 5-1

Percents, Fractions, and Decimals

Lesson Objective	Common Core Standard
To convert between fractions, decimals, and percents	Expressions and Equations: 7.EE.3

Key Concepts

Fractions, Decimals, and Percents

You can write 21 out of 100 as a fraction, a decimal, or a percent.

Fraction	Decimal	Percent

Examples

❶ **Writing Decimals as Percents** Write 0.101, .008, and 2.012 as percents.

$0.101 = \dfrac{101}{\boxed{}}$ $0.008 = \dfrac{8}{\boxed{}}$ $2.012 = \dfrac{2{,}012}{\boxed{}}$ ← **Write as a fraction.**

$= \dfrac{\boxed{}}{\boxed{}}$ $= \dfrac{\boxed{}}{\boxed{}}$ $= \dfrac{\boxed{}}{\boxed{}}$ ← **Write an equivalent fraction with $\boxed{}$ in the denominator.**

$= \boxed{}$ $= \boxed{}$ $= \boxed{}$ ← **Write as a percent.**

❷ **Writing Percents as Decimals** Write 6.4%, .07%, and 3250% as decimals.

$6.4\% = \dfrac{\boxed{}}{\boxed{}}$ $0.07\% = \dfrac{\boxed{}}{\boxed{}}$ $3250\% = \dfrac{\boxed{}}{\boxed{}}$ ← **Write the percent as a fraction.**

$= \boxed{}$ $= \boxed{}$ $= \boxed{}$ ← **Divide.**

Quick Check

1. Write 0.607, 0.005, and 9.283 as percents.

$\boxed{}$ $\boxed{}$ $\boxed{}$

2. Write each percent as a decimal.

a. 3500% $\boxed{}$ **b.** 12.5% $\boxed{}$ **c.** 0.78% $\boxed{}$

Examples

❸ Writing Percents as Fractions Write each percent as a fraction in simplest form.

a. 12% **b.** 45%

$$12\% = \dfrac{12}{\boxed{}}$$ ← Write as a fraction with a denominator of $\boxed{}$. → $$45\% = \dfrac{45}{\boxed{}}$$

$$= \dfrac{12 \div \boxed{}}{100 \div \boxed{}}$$ ← Divide the numerator and the denominator by the GCF. → $$= \dfrac{45 \div \boxed{}}{100 \div \boxed{}}$$

$$= \dfrac{\boxed{}}{\boxed{}}$$ ← Simplify the fraction. → $$= \dfrac{\boxed{}}{\boxed{}}$$

❹ Ordering Rational Numbers Order $\dfrac{3}{5}, \dfrac{2}{10}, 0.645$, and 13% from least to greatest. Write all numbers as decimals. Then graph each number on a number line.

$\dfrac{3}{5} = \boxed{}$ ← Divide the $\boxed{}$ by the $\boxed{}$.

$\dfrac{2}{10} = \boxed{}$ ← Divide the $\boxed{}$ by the $\boxed{}$.

0.645 ← This number is already in decimal form.

$13\% = \boxed{}$ ← Move the decimal point $\boxed{}$ places to the $\boxed{}$.

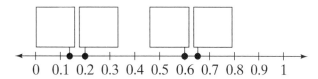

Quick Check

3. An elephant eats about 6% of its body weight in vegetation every day. Write this as a fraction in simplest form.

4. Order from least to greatest.

a. $\dfrac{3}{10}, 0.74, 29\%, \dfrac{11}{25}$ **b.** $15\%, \dfrac{7}{20}, 0.08, 500\%$

Lesson 5-2

Solving Percent Problems Using Proportions

Lesson Objective	Common Core Standard
To use proportions to solve problems involving percent	Ratios and Proportions: 7.RP.3

Key Concepts

Percents and Proportions

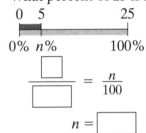
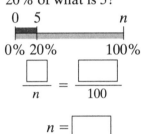

Finding a Percent
What percent of 25 is 5?

0   5   25

0% n%   100%

$$\frac{\boxed{}}{\boxed{}} = \frac{n}{100}$$

$$n = \boxed{}$$

Finding a Part
What is 20% of 25?

0   n 25

0% 20%   100%

$$\frac{n}{\boxed{}} = \frac{\boxed{}}{100}$$

$$n = \boxed{}$$

Finding a Whole
20% of what is 5?

0   5 n

0% 20%   100%

$$\frac{\boxed{}}{n} = \frac{\boxed{}}{100}$$

$$n = \boxed{}$$

Example

❶ Finding a Percent What percent of 150 is 45?
You can write a proportion to find the percent.

$$\frac{45}{\boxed{}} = \frac{n}{\boxed{}} \qquad \leftarrow \text{Write a proportion.}$$

$$\boxed{}\, n = 45\left(\boxed{}\right) \qquad \leftarrow \text{Write the cross products.}$$

$$\frac{150n}{\boxed{}} = \frac{45(100)}{\boxed{}} \qquad \leftarrow \text{Divide each side by } \boxed{}.$$

$$n = \boxed{} \qquad \leftarrow \text{Simplify.}$$

45 is $\boxed{}$ % of 150.

Quick Check

1. What percent of 92 is 23?

Examples

❷ Finding a Part 24% of 25 is what number?

$$\frac{n}{\boxed{}} = \frac{\boxed{}}{100} \quad \leftarrow \textbf{Write a proportion.}$$

$$\frac{n}{\boxed{}} = \frac{\boxed{}}{25} \quad \leftarrow \textbf{Simplify the fraction.}$$

$$n = \boxed{} \quad \leftarrow \textbf{Simplify.}$$

$\boxed{}$ is 24% of 25.

❸ Finding the Whole Use a proportion to answer the question: 117 is 45% of what number?

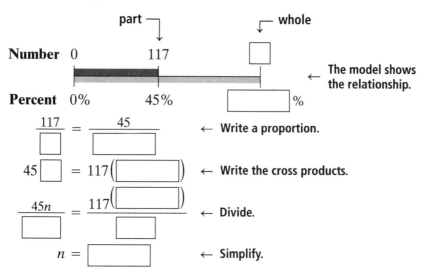

$$\frac{117}{\boxed{}} = \frac{45}{\boxed{}} \quad \leftarrow \textbf{Write a proportion.}$$

$$45\,\boxed{} = 117\left(\boxed{}\right) \quad \leftarrow \textbf{Write the cross products.}$$

$$\frac{45n}{\boxed{}} = \frac{117\left(\boxed{}\right)}{\boxed{}} \quad \leftarrow \textbf{Divide.}$$

$$n = \boxed{} \quad \leftarrow \textbf{Simplify.}$$

Quick Check

2. 85% of 20 is what number?

$$\boxed{}$$

3. Your math teacher assigns 25 problems for homework. You have done 60% of them. How many problems have you done?

$$\boxed{}$$

Name _____ Class _____ Date _____

Lesson 5-3   Solving Percent Problems Using Equations

Lesson Objective	Common Core Standard
To use equations to solve problems involving percent	Ratios and Proportions: 7.RP.3

Key Concepts

Percents and Proportions

Finding a Percent

What percent of 25 is 5?

$n \cdot \boxed{} = \boxed{}$

$n = \boxed{}$

5 is $\boxed{}$ of 25.

Finding a Part

What is 20% of 25?

$n = \boxed{} \cdot \boxed{}$

$n = \boxed{}$

$\boxed{}$ is 20% of 25.

Finding a Whole

20% of what is 5?

$\boxed{} \cdot n = \boxed{}$

$n = \boxed{}$

20% of $\boxed{}$ is 5.

Examples

1 **Finding a Whole** In a school election, one candidate received 81 votes. This was 18% of the votes counted. How many votes were counted?

A. 45 **B.** 145 **C.** 450 **D.** 1450

Words $\boxed{18\%}$ of $\boxed{\text{the number of votes}}$ is $\boxed{81}$.

Let n = the number of votes counted.

Equation $\boxed{} \cdot \boxed{} = \boxed{}$

$\boxed{} \cdot \boxed{} = \boxed{}$ ← Write the equation.

$\dfrac{0.18n}{\boxed{}} = \dfrac{81}{\boxed{}}$ ← Divide each side by $\boxed{}$.

$n = \boxed{}$ ← Simplify.

$\boxed{}$ votes were counted. The correct choice answer is $\boxed{}$.

2 **Finding a Part** What number is 32% of 40?

Words $\boxed{\text{A number}}$ is $\boxed{32\%}$ of $\boxed{40}$.

Let $\boxed{}$ = the number.

Equation $\boxed{} = \boxed{} \cdot \boxed{}$

$= \boxed{}$ ← Simplify.

Name _____ Class _____ Date _____

Example

❸ **Finding a Percent** Of the 257 sandwiches sold at a delicatessen one day, 45 were turkey sandwiches. What percent of the sandwiches were turkey?

Estimate About 50 of 250 sandwiches were turkey.

$$\frac{\boxed{}}{\boxed{}} = \frac{\boxed{}}{\boxed{}} = \boxed{}\%$$

$\boxed{} \cdot \boxed{} = \boxed{}$ ← Write an equation. Let $p =$ the percent of sandwiches that are turkey.

$\dfrac{257p}{\boxed{}} = \dfrac{45}{\boxed{}}$ ← Divide each side by $\boxed{}$.

$p \approx \boxed{}$ ← Use a calculator.

$p \approx \boxed{}\%$ ← Write the decimal as a percent.

Check for Reasonableness $\boxed{}$% is close to the estimate $\boxed{}$%.

Quick Check

1. A plane flies with 54% of its seats empty. If 81 seats are empty, what is the total number of seats on the plane?

2. 27% of 60 is what number?

3. It rained 75 days last year. About what percent of the year was rainy?

Lesson 5-4

Applications of Percent

Lesson Objective	Common Core Standard
To find and estimate solutions to application problems involving percent and to use different ways to represent a situation	Ratios and Proportions: 7.RP.3

Examples

1 **Finding Sales Tax** A video game costs $34.98. The sales tax rate is 5.5%. How much will you pay for the video game?

[____] · 34.98 ≈ [____] ← **Find the sales tax. Round to the nearest cent.**

34.98 + [____] = [____] ← **Add the sales tax to the purchase price.**

You will pay [____] for the video game.

2 **Estimating a Tip** Use estimation to calculate a 15% tip for $34.50.

34.50 ≈ [____] ← **Round to the nearest dollar.**

0.1 · [____] = [____] ← **Find 10% of the bill.**

$\frac{1}{2}$ · [____] = [____] ← **Find 5% of the bill. 5% is $\frac{1}{2}$ of the 10% amount.**

[____] + [____] = [____] ← **Add 10% amount and 5% amount to get [____].**

A 15% tip for $34.50 is about [____].

3 **Finding a Commission** Find the commission on a $300 sale, with a commission rate of 8.5%.

[____] · [____] = [____] ← **Write 8.5% as [____] and multiply.**

The commission on the sale is [____].

Quick Check

1. Find the total cost for a purchase of $185 if the sales tax rate is 5.5%.

[_____]

2. Estimate a 15% tip for each amount.
   a. $58.20   **b.** $61.80   **c.** $49.75

[_____]   [_____]   [_____]

3. Find the commission on a $3,200 sale, with a commission rate of 6%.

[_____]

Name _____ Class _____ Date _____

Examples

④ Finding a Commission Find the total earnings for a salesperson with a salary of $550 plus 4% commission on sales of $1,485.

Words $\boxed{\text{total earnings}} = \boxed{\text{salary}} + \boxed{\text{commission}}$.

Let t = total earnings.

Equation $\boxed{} = \boxed{} + \boxed{} \cdot \boxed{}$

$t = \boxed{} + \boxed{} \cdot \boxed{}$ ← **Write the equation.**

$= 550 + \boxed{}$ ← **Multiply.**

$= \boxed{}$ ← **Simplify.**

The salesperson earns $\boxed{}$.

⑤ Application: Percent Error in Manufacturing

A 625-g mass measures 625.18 g. What is the percent error?

$$\text{Percent Error} = \frac{\text{Actual Value} - \boxed{}}{\text{Actual Value}} \cdot 100$$

$$\text{Percent Error} = \frac{\boxed{} - \boxed{}}{625} \cdot 100 \quad \leftarrow \textbf{Use decimals in the formula.}$$

$$= \frac{\boxed{}}{\boxed{}} \cdot 100 \quad \leftarrow \textbf{Find the absolute value.}$$

$$= \boxed{} \cdot 100 \quad \leftarrow \textbf{Simplify the fraction.}$$

$$= \boxed{} \quad \leftarrow \textbf{Multiply. Round to the nearest hundredth.}$$

The percent error is $\boxed{}$ %.

Quick Check

4. Suppose you earn a weekly salary of $800 plus a commission of 3.5% on all sales. Find your earnings for a week with total sales of $1,400.

5. At a sporting goods factory, a quality control technician checking the weights of baseball bats measures a bat that should weigh 26 oz at $26\frac{1}{4}$ oz. If a bat is not within 0.6% of its specified weight, it is rejected. Why does this bat pass or fail this test?

Lesson 5-5

Simple Interest

Lesson Objective	Common Core Standard
To find simple interest	Ratios and Proportions: 7.RP.3

Vocabulary and Key Concept

Simple Interest Formula

$$I = \boxed{}$$

I is the interest earned, *p* is the principal, *r* is the interest rate per year, and *t* is the time in years.

Principal is _____

_____

Simple interest is _____

_____

Examples

❶ **Finding Simple Interest** You invest $500 at a 3% annual interest rate for 4 years. What is the simple interest earned in dollars?

$I = prt$ ← **Write the formula.**

$I = (500)\left(\boxed{}\right)\left(\boxed{}\right)$ ← **Substitute. Use** $\boxed{}$ **for 3%.**

$= \boxed{}$ ← **Simplify.**

The interest is $\boxed{}$.

❷ **Graphing Simple Interest** You have $500 in an account that earns an annual rate of 3%. At the end of each year, you withdraw the interest you have earned. Graph the total interest you earn after 1, 2, 3, and 4 years.

Step 1 Make a table.

Time (yr)	Interest ($)
1	15
2	
3	
4	

Step 2 Draw a graph.

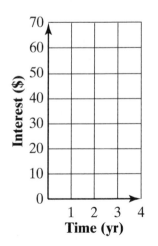

Example

❸ **Comparing Loans** You need to borrow $2,000. There is a 4-year loan with a 6% simple interest and a 2-year loan with a 11% simple interest. Which loan will cost more?

4 Year Loan	2 Year Loan	
$I = prt$	$I = prt$	← **Write the formula.**
$I = 2,000 \cdot \boxed{} \cdot \boxed{}$	$I = 2,000 \cdot \boxed{} \cdot \boxed{}$	← **Substitute.**
$I = \boxed{}$	$I = \boxed{}$	← **Simplify.**
$\boxed{} > \boxed{}$		← **Compare.**

The $\boxed{}$-year loan will cost more.

Quick Check

1. Find the simple interest you pay on a $220 loan at a 5% annual interest rate for 4 years.

2. Graph the simple interest earned on $950 at an annual rate of 4.2%.

3. Barbara wants to borrow $2000. She can get a loan of $2000 at 7% simple interest for 3 years or at 11% simple interest for 2 years. Which loan will cost her more?

Name _____ Class _____ Date _____

Lesson 5-6

Finding Percent of Change

Lesson Objective	Common Core Standards
To find percents of increase and percents of decrease	Ratios and Proportions: 7.RP.3 Expressions and Equations: 7.EE.2

Vocabulary

The percent of change is _____

_____

A markup is _____

_____

A discount is _____

_____

Example

1 Finding a Percent of Increase Last year, a school had 632 students. This year the school has 670 students. Find the percent of increase in the number of students.

$670 - 632 = \boxed{}$ ← **Find the amount of change.**

$\dfrac{38}{\boxed{}} = \dfrac{n}{\boxed{}}$ ← **Write a proportion. Let n = percent of change.**

$100 \cdot \dfrac{38}{\boxed{}} = \dfrac{n}{\boxed{}} \cdot 100$ ← **Multiply each side by 100.**

$\dfrac{3800}{\boxed{}} = n$ ← **Simplify.**

$n \approx \boxed{}$ ← **Divide.**

The number of students increased by about $\boxed{}$.

Quick Check

1. In 2010, Georgia went from 13 to 14 representatives. Find the percent of increase in the number of representatives.

_____

Examples

❷ **Finding a Percent of Markup** Find the percent of markup for a car that a dealer buys for $10,590 and sells for $13,775.

$13,775 - 10,590 = \boxed{}$ ← **Find the amount of markup.**

$\dfrac{3,185}{\boxed{}} = \dfrac{n}{\boxed{}}$ ← **Write a proportion. Let *n* be the percent of markup.**

$\boxed{}\, n = \boxed{}(100)$ ← **Write cross products.**

$\dfrac{\boxed{}\, n}{\boxed{}} = \dfrac{\boxed{}(100)}{\boxed{}}$ ← **Divide each side by** $\boxed{}$.

$n \approx \boxed{}$ ← **Simplify.**

The percent of markup is about $\boxed{}$.

❸ **Finding a Percent of Discount** Find the percent of discount for a $74.99 tent that is discounted to $48.75.

$74.99 - 48.75 = \boxed{}$ ← **Find the amount of the discount.**

$\dfrac{26.24}{\boxed{}} = \dfrac{n}{\boxed{}}$ ← **Write a proportion. Let *n* be the percent of discount.**

$\boxed{}\, n = 26.24\left(\boxed{}\right)$ ← **Write cross products.**

$\dfrac{\boxed{}\, n}{\boxed{}} = \dfrac{26.24\left(\boxed{}\right)}{\boxed{}}$ ← **Divide each side by** $\boxed{}$.

$n \approx \boxed{}$ ← **Simplify.**

The percent of discount for the tent is about $\boxed{}$.

Quick Check

2. Find the percent of markup for a $17.95 headset marked up to $35.79.

3. Find the percent of discount of a $24.95 novel on sale for $14.97.

Lesson 6-1

Lesson Objective	Common Core Standard
To write and solve equations to find unknown angle measures	Geometry: 7.G.5

Vocabulary

An angle is _____

_____

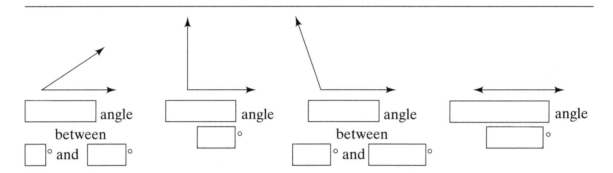

[_____] angle   [_____] angle   [_____] angle   [_____] angle
between   [___]°   between   [___]°
[___]° and [___]°   [___]° and [___]°

Adjacent angles are _____   Circle an angle
                                                         adjacent to ∠1.
_____

Vertical angles are _____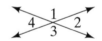

_____

If the sum of the measure of two angles is 90°, the angles   Circle an vertical
are [_____] . If the sum is 180°, the angles   angle to ∠1.

are [_____] .

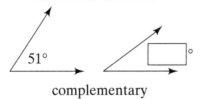

51°   [_____]°   65°   [_____]°

complementary   supplementary

Congruent angles are _____

_____

Name _____ Class _____ Date _____

Examples

① **Finding Supplements and Complements** Write and solve an equation to find the measures of the two angles described at the right.

$6x + (19x + 5) = 180$ ← **The angles are supplementary.**

$\left(6x + \boxed{}\right) + 5 = 180$ ← **Use the** $\boxed{}$ **Property.**

$\boxed{} + 5 = 180$ ← **Combine like terms.**

$\boxed{} + 5 - \boxed{} = 180 - \boxed{}$ ← **Subtract** $\boxed{}$ **from each side.**

$\boxed{} = \boxed{}$ ← **Simplify.**

$\dfrac{\boxed{}}{\boxed{}} = \dfrac{175}{\boxed{}}$ ← **Divide.**

$x = 7$ ← **Simplify.**

Calculate the angle measures.

$6\left(\boxed{}\right) = \boxed{}$ and $19\left(\boxed{}\right) + 5 = \boxed{}$

The angle measures are $\boxed{}°$ and $\boxed{}°$.

② **Finding Angle Measures** In the diagram, $m\angle 3 = 32°$. Find the measures of $\angle 1$, $\angle 2$, and $\angle 4$.

$m\angle 2 + 32° = \boxed{}$ ← $\angle$**2 and** $\angle$**3 are** $\boxed{}$.

$m\angle 2 + 32° - 32° = \boxed{} - 32°$ ← **Subtract 32° from each side.**

$m\angle 2 = \boxed{}$ ← **Simplify.**

$m\angle 1 = \boxed{}$ ← $\angle$**1 and** $\angle$**3 are** $\boxed{}$ **angles.**

$m\angle 4 = \boxed{}$ ← $\angle$**2 and** $\angle$**4 are** $\boxed{}$ **angles.**

Quick Check

1. Write and solve an equation to find the measures of the two angles described at the right. $\boxed{}$

2. In the diagram at the right, $m\angle 8 = 72°$. Find the measures of $\angle 5$, $\angle 6$, and $\angle 7$.

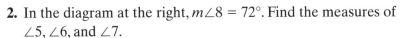

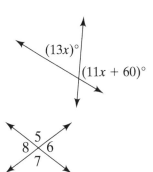

Daily Notetaking Guide   *Course 2* Lesson 6-1   **65**

Lesson 6-2

Lesson Objective	Common Core Standard
To find the area of a parallelogram and to relate perimeter and area	Equations and Expressions: 7.G.6

Vocabulary and Key Concepts

Area of a Parallelogram

The area of a parallelogram is equal to the product of any ⬚ b and the corresponding ⬚ h.

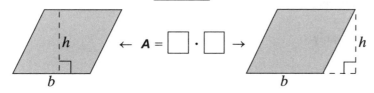

$\leftarrow A = \boxed{} \cdot \boxed{} \rightarrow$

The height of a parallelogram is _____

_____

_____

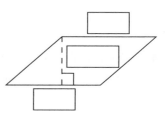

Examples

❶ Finding the Area of a Parallelogram Find the area of the parallelogram.

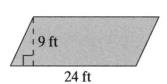

9 ft

24 ft

$A = \boxed{}\boxed{}$ ← **Use the area formula.**

$= (\boxed{})(\boxed{})$ ← **Substitute.**

$= \boxed{}$ ← **Simplify.**

The area is $\boxed{}$ ft^2.

❷ Relating Perimeter and Area Jacob wants to fence in a rectangular dog run in his back yard. He has 46 feet of fencing and wants the dog run to be as large as possible. Which dimensions should he use?

A. length of 9 ft and width of 14 ft   B. length of 10 ft and width of 14 ft
C. length of 11 ft and width of 12 ft   D. length of 12 ft and width of 12 ft

Since all answer choices give the length *l* and the width *w*, you can calculate both the perimeter $2l + 2w$, and the area [____].

Perimeter   **Area**

[__] (9) + [__] (14) = [__]   [__][__][__] = [__]   ← Perimeter is correct; find the area.

[__] (10) + [__] (14) = [__]   ← Perimeter is greater than 46 ft.

[__] (11) + [__] (12) = [__]   [__][__][__] = [__]   ← Perimeter is correct; the area in choice A is [____].

[__] (12) + [__] (12) = [__]   ← Perimeter is greater than 46 ft.

The rectangle with a length of [__] ft and a width of [__] ft will have the correct perimeter and the greatest area. The correct answer is choice [__].

Quick Check

1. Find the area of the parallelogram.

[_____]

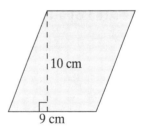
10 cm
9 cm

2. What is the perimeter of the rectangle?

[_____]

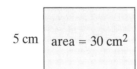
5 cm | area = 30 cm²

Lesson 6-3

Area of a Triangle

Lesson Objective	Common Core Standard
To find the area of a triangle and to relate side lengths and area	Geometry: 7.G.6

Vocabulary and Key Concepts

Area of a Triangle

The area of a triangle is equal to half the product of any

[ ] and the corresponding [ ].

$A = \frac{1}{2}$ [ ] [ ]

The height of a triangle _____

_____

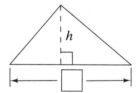

Examples

1 **Finding the Area of a Triangle** Find the area of each triangle.

a.

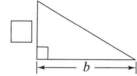

$A = \frac{1}{2}$ [ ] [ ] ← Use the area formula.

$\quad = \frac{1}{2}$ ([ ])([ ]) ← Substitute.

$\quad = $ [ ] ← Simplify.

The area is [ ] yd².

b. The triangle has side lengths of 16.2 cm, 15.4 cm, and 2.4 cm. Draw the height going to the base of length 2.4 cm. The height is 15 cm.

$A = $ [ ] bh ← Use the area formula.

$\quad = $ [ ] [ ] [ ] ← Substitute.

$\quad = $ [ ] ← Simplify.

The area is [ ] cm².

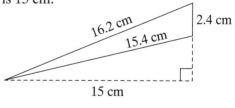

Name _____ Class _____ Date _____

❷ Relating Side Lengths and Area Triangle A below has sides three times as long as the sides of Triangle B. How does the area of Triangle A compare to the area of Triangle B?

Triangle A

$b = \boxed{}$ in., $h = \boxed{}$ in.

$A = \frac{1}{2}\left(\boxed{}\right)\left(\boxed{}\right)$

$= \boxed{}$

Triangle B

$b = \boxed{}$ in.; $h = \boxed{}$ in.

$A = \frac{1}{2}\left(\boxed{}\right)\left(\boxed{}\right)$

$= \boxed{}$

The area of Triangle A is $\boxed{}$ in^2. The area of Triangle B is $\boxed{}$ in^2. So, the area of Triangle A is $\boxed{}$ times greater than the area of Triangle B.

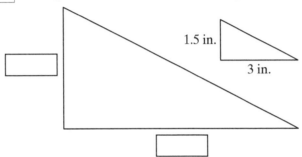

1.5 in.

3 in.

Quick Check

1. Find the area of each triangle.

a.

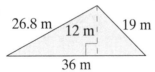

26.8 m   12 m   19 m

36 m

b.

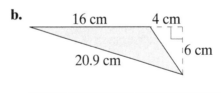

16 cm   4 cm

20.9 cm

6 cm

2. What is the unknown side length of the triangle? $\boxed{}$

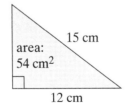

15 cm

area:
54 cm^2

12 cm

Lesson 6-4

Areas of Other Figures

Lesson Objective	Common Core Standard
To find the area of a trapezoid and the areas of irregular figures	Equations and Expressions: 7.G.6

Vocabulary and Key Concepts

Area of a Trapezoid

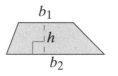

The area of a trapezoid is [ ] the product of the [ ] and the sum of the lengths of the [ ].

$$A = \frac{1}{2}\square(\square + \square)$$

If you put two identical trapezoids together, you get a parallelogram. The area of the parallelogram is [ ].
The area of one trapezoid is [ ].

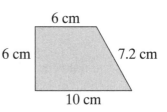

The bases of a trapezoid are _____

The height of a trapezoid is _____

_____

Examples

❶ **Finding the Area of a Trapezoid** Find the area of the trapezoid.

$A = \frac{1}{2}\square(\square + \square)$ ← Use the area formula for a trapezoid.

$= \frac{1}{2}(\square)(\square + \square)$ ← Substitute for h, b_1, and b_2.

$= \frac{1}{2}(\square)(16)$ ← Add.

$= \square$ ← Multiply.

The area is $\square$ cm².

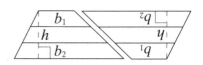

❷ Geography Estimate the area of the figure by finding the area of the trapezoid.

$A = \frac{1}{2}\boxed{}\left(\boxed{} + b_2\right)$ ← **Use the area formula for a trapezoid.**

$= \frac{1}{2}\left(\boxed{}\right)\left(\boxed{} + \boxed{}\right)$ ← **Substitute for h, b_1, and b_2.**

$= \frac{1}{2}\left(\boxed{}\right)\left(\boxed{}\right)$ ← **Add.**

$= \boxed{}$ ← **Multiply.**

The area of the figure is about $\boxed{}$ ft^2.

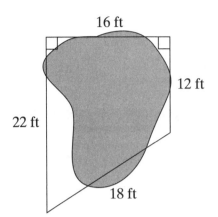

16 ft

12 ft

22 ft

18 ft

Quick Check

1. Find the area of each trapezoid.

a.

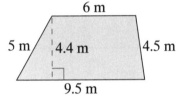

6 m

5 m 4.4 m 4.5 m

9.5 m

$\boxed{}$ m^2

b.

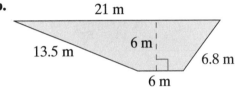

21 m

13.5 m 6 m 6.8 m

6 m

$\boxed{}$ m^2

2. Estimate the area of the figure by finding the area of the trapezoid.

$\boxed{}$

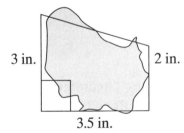

3 in. 2 in.

3.5 in.

Lesson 6-5

Circumference and Area of a Circle

Lesson Objective	Common Core Standard
To find the circumference and area of a circle	Equations and Expressions: 7.G.4

Vocabulary and Key Concepts

Circumference of a Circle

The circumference of a circle is ☐ times the ☐☐☐ .

$$C = \pi d = 2\pi r$$

Area of a Circle

The area of a circle is the product of ☐ and the square of the ☐☐ .

$$A = \pi r^2$$

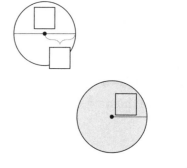

Circumference is _____

_____

Pi (π) is _____

_____

Examples

❶ **Finding the Circumference of a Circle** Find the circumference of each circle. Round to the nearest tenth.

a.

9 yd

$C = \boxed{}$

$= 2\pi \left(\boxed{}\right)$

$= \boxed{}$

← Use the formula for circumference. →
← Substitute. →
← Use a calculator. →

The circumference is approximately ☐ yd.

b.

40 cm

$C = \boxed{}$

$= \pi \left(\boxed{}\right)$

$= \boxed{}$

The circumference is approximately ☐ cm.

Daily Notetaking Guide

❷ Finding the Area of a Circle A pizza has a diameter of 28 cm. What is the area of the pizza? Round to the nearest tenth.

$r = \dfrac{\boxed{}}{2} = \boxed{}$ ← **The radius is half the diameter.**

$A = \boxed{}$ ← **Use the formula for the area of a circle.**

$= \pi \left(\boxed{} \right)^2$ ← **Substitute** $\boxed{}$ **for the radius.**

$\approx \boxed{}$ ← **Use a calculator.**

$\approx \boxed{}$ ← **Round the solution to the nearest tenth.**

The area of the pizza is approximately $\boxed{}$ cm^2.

Quick Check

1. Find the circumference of the circle. Round to the nearest tenth.

9 m $\boxed{}$ m

2. Find the area of the circle. Round to the nearest square unit.

12 m $\boxed{}$ m^2

Lesson 7-1

Three-Dimensional Figures

Lesson Objective	
To classify and draw three-dimensional figures	

Vocabulary

A three-dimensional figure, or solid, is _____
_____

A face is _____
_____

An edge is _____
_____

A prism is _____
_____

The bases of a prism are _____

The height of a prism is _____
_____

Prism

A cube is _____

A ⬚ has two congruent parallel ⬚ that are ⬚.

The height of a cylinder is _____
_____

A ⬚ has ⬚ faces that meet at one point,
a ⬚ , and a base that is a ⬚ .

A ⬚ has one circular ⬚ and
one ⬚ .

A ⬚ is the set of all points in space that are the same
distance from a ⬚ point.

Examples

1 **Naming Figures** Name the geometric figure.

The figure is a [   ] .

2 **Drawing Three-Dimensional Figures** Draw a pentagonal prism.

Step 1 Draw a [   ] .

Step 2 Draw a second [   ] congruent to the first.

Step 3 Connect the vertices. Use [   ] for hidden edges.

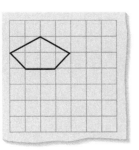

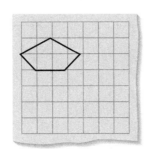

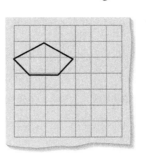

Quick Check

1. Name each figure.

a.

[   ]

b.

[   ]

2. Use the grid to draw a triangular prism.

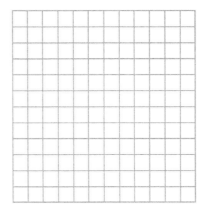

Lesson 7-2

Surface Areas of Prisms and Cylinders

Lesson Objective	Common Core Standard
To find the surface areas of prisms and cylinders using nets	Geometry: 7.G.6

Vocabulary

A net is _____

The surface area of a prism is _____

Example

1 **Drawing a Net** Draw a net for the cube.

 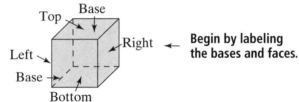

Begin by labeling the bases and faces.

First, draw one base. Then, draw one face that connects both bases.
Next, draw the other base. Draw and label the remaining faces.

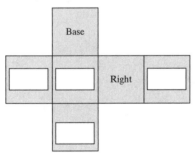

Quick Check

1. Draw a different net for the cube in Example 1.

Examples

② **Finding the Surface Area of a Prism** Find the surface area of the prism.

First, draw a net for the prism.

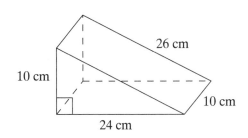

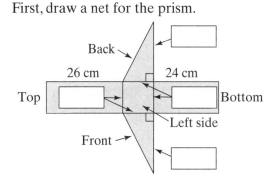

Then, find the total area of the five faces.

top   bottom   left side   front side   back side

$10(\boxed{}) + 10(\boxed{}) + 10(\boxed{}) + \frac{1}{2}(\boxed{})(\boxed{}) + \frac{1}{2}(\boxed{})(\boxed{}) = \boxed{}$

The surface area of the triangular prism is $\boxed{}$ cm².

③ **Finding the Surface Area of a Cylinder** Find the surface area of the cylinder. Round to the nearest tenth.

Step 1 Draw a net.

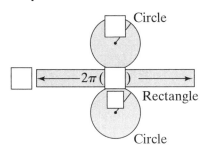

Step 2 Find the area of one circle.

$A = \pi r^2$

$= \pi \left(\boxed{}\right)^2$

$= \pi \left(\boxed{}\right)$

$\approx \boxed{}$

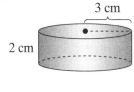

Step 3 Find the area of the rectangle.

$(2\pi r)\boxed{} = 2\pi(3)\left(\boxed{}\right) = \boxed{} \pi \approx \boxed{}$ cm²

Step 4 Add the areas of the two circles and the rectangle.

Surface Area = $\boxed{} + \boxed{} + \boxed{} = \boxed{}$

The surface area of the cylinder is about $\boxed{}$ cm².

Quick Check

2. Find the surface area of the rectangular prism.

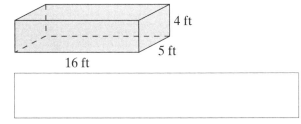

3. What is the surface area of the cylinder? Round to the nearest tenth.

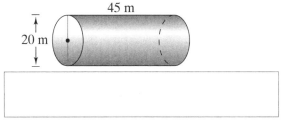

Lesson 7-3

Volumes of Prisms and Cylinders

Lesson Objective	Common Core Standard
To find the volume of prisms and cylinders	Geometry: 7.G.6

Vocabulary and Key Concepts

Volume of a Rectangular Prism

V = area of base · [＿＿＿]

= Bh

= [＿＿＿]

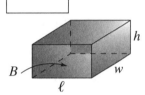

Volume of a Triangular Prism

V = area of base · height

= Bh

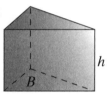

Volume of a Cylinder

V = area of base · [＿＿＿]

= Bh

= [＿＿＿]

The volume of a three-dimensional figure is _____

_____

A cubic unit is _____

Examples

1 **Finding the Volume of a Rectangular Prism** Find the volume of the rectangular prism.

V = [＿＿＿]   ← **Use the formula.**

= ([＿]) ([＿]) ([＿])   ← **Substitute.**

= [＿＿＿]   ← **Multiply.**

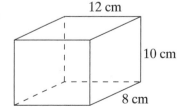

The volume of the rectangular prism is [＿＿] cm³.

❷ Finding the Volume of a Triangular Prism Find the volume of the triangular prism.

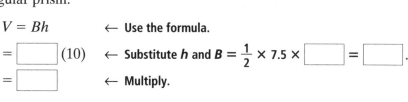

7.5 in. 10 in.

10 in.

12.5 in.

$V = Bh$ ← **Use the formula.**

$= \boxed{}(10)$ ← **Substitute h and $B = \frac{1}{2} \times 7.5 \times \boxed{} = \boxed{}$.**

$= \boxed{}$ ← **Multiply.**

The volume of the triangular prism is $\boxed{}$ cubic inches.

❸ Finding the Volume of a Cylinder A glass is 7.4 cm tall. The base of the glass has a diameter of 2.2 cm. Estimate the volume that the glass can hold if it is filled to the top. Then find the volume to the nearest cubic unit that the glass can hold if it is filled to the top.

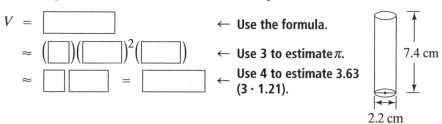

$V = \boxed{}$ ← **Use the formula.**

$\approx (\boxed{})(\boxed{})^2(\boxed{})$ ← **Use 3 to estimate π.**

$\approx \boxed{}\boxed{} = \boxed{}$ ← **Use 4 to estimate 3.63 (3 · 1.21).**

7.4 cm

2.2 cm

The estimated volume is $\boxed{}$ cm^3.

Calculated volume: $V = \pi(\boxed{})^2(\boxed{}) \approx \boxed{}$.   ← **Use a calculator.**

The calculated volume is about $\boxed{}$ cm^3.   ← **Round to the nearest whole number.**

Quick Check

1. If the height of the prism in Example 1 is doubled, what is the volume?

$\boxed{}$

2. If the height of the prism in Example 2 is doubled, what is the volume?

$\boxed{}$

3. Estimate the volume of the cylinder. Then, find the volume to the nearest cubic centimeter.

24 cm

18 cm

Lesson 7-4

Cross Sections

Lesson Objective	Common Core Standard
To describe and draw cross sections that result from slicing three-dimensional figures	Geometry: 7.G.3

Vocabulary

If you slice through a three-dimensional object like this pyramid, you see a two-dimensional shape called a [   ] of the solid.

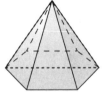

Example

1 **Identifying a Cross Section** Jordan uses foam blocks in the shape of a triangular prism as props for the school play. He slices one block vertically. He slices another block horizontally. Describe the shape of each cross section.

a.

Vertical Slice

The vertical slice creates a triangular cross section.

b.

Horizontal Slice

The horizontal slice creates a rectangular cross section.

Quick Check

1. Jorge and Patti are eating sushi rolls shaped like cylinders. Jorge cut his sushi roll vertically. Patti cut her sushi roll horizontally. What is the shape of each cross section?

a. Jorge

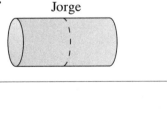

b. Patti

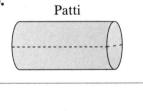

Example

❷ **Describing a Cross Section** A carpenter is cutting wooden blocks in two ways. He slices some blocks with a vertical cut, from one corner diagonally to the opposite corner. He cuts other blocks horizontally. Draw and describe the cross section formed by the saw cutting the blocks of wood.

a. Vertical Cut

The saw will create a rectangular cross section with length equal to a line diagonally across the block width equal to the block's height.

b. Horizontal Cut

The saw will create a rectangular cross section with length equal to the length of the block and width equal to the block's width.

Quick Check

2. Describe the cross section formed by the slices through the hexagonal pyramid.

a.

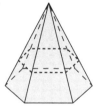

b.

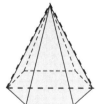

c. Reasoning Would any other slices through the pyramid produce a different type of cross section? If so, describe how the slice would have to be made.

_____

_____

Lesson 8-1

Lesson Objective	Common Core Standard
To identify a random sample and to write a survey question	Statistics and Probability: 7.SP.1

Vocabulary

A population is _____

A sample is _____

A random sample is _____

_____

A biased question is _____

_____

Example

❶ **Identifying a Random Sample** You survey students in your school about their snacking habits. Would you get a random sample if you questioned different English classes? Explain.

Quick Check

1. You survey a store's customers. You ask why they chose the store. Which sample is more likely to be random? Explain.

   a. You survey 20 people at the entrance from 5:00 P.M. to 8:00 P.M.

   b. You survey 20 people outside the entrance throughout the day.

Example

❷ **Identifying Biased Questions** Is each question *biased* or *fair*? Explain.

a. "Which is a brighter color, pink, or green?"

This question is ▯. The choices are presented equally.

b. "Is an electric pink shirt brighter than a green shirt?"

This question is ▯. It implies that pink is brighter, thus influencing the responses.

Quick Check

2. Is each question *biased* or *fair*? Explain.

a. Do you prefer greasy meat or healthy vegetables on your pizza?

b. Which pizza topping do you like best?

Lesson 8-2

Lesson Objective	Common Core Standard
To estimate population size using proportions	Statistics and Probability: 7.SP.2

Vocabulary

The capture/recapture method is used to _____

_____

Example

❶ Using the Capture/Recapture Method Researchers know that there are 63 marked gazelles in an area. On a flight over the area, they count 19 marked gazelles and a total of 412 gazelles. Write a proportion to estimate the gazelle population.

$$\dfrac{\text{number of marked gazelles counted}}{\text{total number of gazelles counted}} = \dfrac{\text{total number of marked gazelles}}{\text{estimate of gazelle population}}$$

$$\dfrac{\boxed{}}{\boxed{}} = \dfrac{63}{x} \qquad \leftarrow \textbf{Write a proportion.}$$

$$19x = 63 \cdot 412 \qquad \leftarrow \textbf{Write cross products.}$$

$$19x = \boxed{} \qquad \leftarrow \textbf{Multiply.}$$

$$\dfrac{19x}{\boxed{}} = \dfrac{25{,}956}{\boxed{}} \qquad \leftarrow \textbf{Divide each side by } \boxed{}.$$

$$x \approx \boxed{} \qquad \leftarrow \textbf{Round to the nearest integer.}$$

There are about $\boxed{}$ gazelles in the area.

Check: You can use an estimate to check your answer.

$$\dfrac{19}{412} \approx \dfrac{\boxed{}}{\boxed{}}, \text{ or } \dfrac{1}{20}$$

$$\dfrac{1}{20} = \dfrac{63}{x}$$

$$x = 63 \times 20 = 1{,}260$$

Since this is close to 1,366, the answer is reasonable.

Quick Check

1. Researchers know that there are 105 marked deer in an area. On a flight over the area, they count 35 marked deer and a total of 638 deer. Estimate the total deer population in the area.

```
┌────────────────────────────────────────────────────────────┐
│                                                              │
│                                                              │
│                                                              │
│                                                              │
└────────────────────────────────────────────────────────────┘
```

Lesson 8-3

Inferences

Lesson Objective	Common Core Standard
To use data from random samples to make inferences about populations	Statistics and Probability: 7.SP.2

Vocabulary

An inference is _____
_____

Example

❶ **Drawing Inferences about a Population** A clothing store selected a random sample of 20 customers and recorded the amount they spent on clothes. Based on the sample, what is the average, or mean, amount that customers spent on clothing?

Step 1 Find the average, or [____], of the sample data.

$$[\quad] = \frac{\text{sum of the data}}{\text{number of data items}}$$

$$= \frac{[\quad]}{[\quad]}$$

$$= [\quad]$$

Random Sample of Amount Spent per Customer ($)				
25	72	10	125	29
96	46	21	17	31
84	63	19	35	9
146	28	57	82	65

Step 2 Use the average of the sample data to make an inference.

The average amount spent by customers in the sample is [____], so the average amount spent by all customers is likely close to [____].

Quick Check

1. A restaurant manager selected a random sample of 20 customers and recorded the amount they spent on their meal. Draw an inference about the percent of customers at the restaurant who spend more than $20.

Random Sample of Amount Spent per Customer ($)				
21	9	23	12	15
16	10	17	17	15
14	16	13	17	17
14	25	14	23	12

_____
_____
_____
_____

Example

2 **Comparing Random Samples** There are 240 workers in a local factory. The factory owner surveys 3 random samples of 25 people each about which new work schedule they would like to adopt. The results are shown in the table.

Schedule	Sample 1	Sample 2	Sample 3
Schedule A	4	7	2
Schedule B	12	10	14
Schedule C	9	8	9

a. For each sample, predict how many votes Schedule B will get.

Use a proportion: $\dfrac{\text{votes for Schedule B in sample}}{\text{people in sample}} = \dfrac{\text{predicted votes for Schedule B}}{\text{people in factory}}$

Sample 1: $\dfrac{12}{25} = \dfrac{x}{240}$

$\boxed{} \cdot 240 = 25x$

$\boxed{} = 25x$

$\boxed{} \approx x$

Sample 2: $\dfrac{10}{25} = \dfrac{x}{240}$

$10 \cdot \boxed{} = 25x$

$\boxed{} = 25x$

$\boxed{} = x$

Sample 3: $\dfrac{14}{25} = \dfrac{x}{240}$

$14 \cdot \boxed{} = 25x$

$\boxed{} = 25x$

$\boxed{} \approx x$

Based on Sample 1, Schedule B will get about $\boxed{}$ votes. Based on Sample 2, Schedule B will get about $\boxed{}$ votes, and based on Sample 3, it will get about $\boxed{}$ votes.

b. Describe the variation in the predictions.

The greatest prediction is $\boxed{}$ votes, and the least prediction is $\boxed{}$ votes. So the predictions vary by $\boxed{} - \boxed{} = \boxed{}$ votes.

c. Make an inference about the number of votes Schedule B will get.

Find the mean of the predictions: $\dfrac{\boxed{}}{3} = \dfrac{\boxed{}}{3} = \boxed{}$.

Schedule B will get about $\boxed{}$ votes.

Quick Check

2. The table shows the results of 3 random samples of 30 students each at a middle school with 420 students. The students were asked how many hours they spend online each week.

Hours Spent Online Per Week

Time (h)	Sample 1	Sample 2	Sample 3
< 5	16	13	11
≥ 5	14	17	19

a. For each sample, predict how many students in the school spend at least 5 hours online per week. _____

b. Describe the variation in the predictions. _____

c. Draw an inference about the number of students in at the school who spend at least 5 hours online per week.

_____

_____

Lesson 8-4

Data Variability

Lesson Objective	Common Core Standards
To compare data about two populations by using measures of center and measures of variability	Statistics and Probability: 7.SP.3, 7.SP.4

Vocabulary

The interquartile range of a set of data is _____

_____

The mean absolute deviation of a data set measures _____

_____

Example

1 **Comparing Two Populations** A gardener collects information about the heights of the flowers she grows. Compare the IQRs of the data sets, and use the comparison to make an inference about the plants.

IQR for Salvia:

[ ] – [ ] = [ ]

IQR for Marigolds:

[ ] – [ ] = [ ]

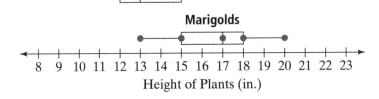

The IQRs of the data sets are [ ] [ ]. So, you can infer that the heights of [ ] vary about as much as the heights of [ ].

Quick Check

1. A veterinarian collects data about the weights of the dogs she treats. Compare the medians of the data sets 1, and use the comparison to make an inference about the plants.

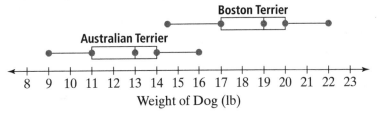

_____

_____

_____

Name _____ Class _____ Date _____

Example

❷ **Determining Overlap of Data Sets** The line plot at the right shows the ages of teens who participated in a junior archery competition.

a. Calculate the mean of each data set.

Girls: Mean = $\dfrac{\boxed{}}{\boxed{}}$ = $\boxed{}$ **Boys:** Mean = $\dfrac{\boxed{}}{\boxed{}}$ = $\boxed{}$

b. Determine the MAD for ages of girls in the competition.

Ages	13	13	14	14	15	15	15	16	17	18
Mean										
Distance										

$$\text{MAD} = \frac{\text{total distance}}{\text{number of data items}} = \frac{\boxed{}}{10} = \frac{\boxed{}}{5} = \boxed{}$$

Participant Ages		
Girls		Boys
✗ ✗	13	✗
✗ ✗	14	
✗ ✗ ✗	15	
✗	16	✗ ✗
✗	17	✗ ✗ ✗
✗	18	✗ ✗
	19	✗ ✗

c. What number n multiplied by the MAD equals the difference between the means? What does this number tell you about the overlap of the data sets?

MAD $\cdot n$ = difference of means ← **Write an equation.**

$1.2n = 17 - \boxed{}$ ← **Substitute.**

$\boxed{}n = \boxed{}$ ← **Simplify.**

$\dfrac{1.2n}{\boxed{}} = \dfrac{2}{\boxed{}}$ ← **Divide each side by** $\boxed{}$**.**

$n = \boxed{}$ ← **Simplify.**

The difference between the means is $\boxed{}$ times the MAD. The multiple $\boxed{}$ is greater than 1, which indicates a $\boxed{}$ amount of overlap in the data sets.

Quick Check

2. The data table at the right shows the number of commercials during a random sample of hour-long shows on two television stations.

a. Calculate the mean of each data set.
Station A: $\boxed{}$ Station B: $\boxed{}$

b. Determine the MAD for Station A commercials. $\boxed{}$

c. What number n multiplied by the MAD equals the difference between the means? $n \approx \boxed{}$.

Commercials During Hour-Long Shows		
Station A		Station B
	32	✗
✗	33	
	34	✗ ✗ ✗
✗ ✗ ✗	35	✗ ✗
✗ ✗ ✗	36	✗ ✗
✗	37	✗ ✗
✗	38	
✗	39	

What does this number tell you about the overlap of the data sets?

_____

_____

Name _____ Class _____ Date _____

Lesson 9-1 Probability

Lesson Objective	Common Core Standards
To find the probability and the complement of an event	Statistics and Probability: 7.SP.5, 7.SP.7.a

Vocabulary and Key Concepts

Theoretical Probability

$$\text{theoretical probability} = P(\text{event}) = \frac{\text{number of } \boxed{} \text{ outcomes}}{\text{total number of } \boxed{} \text{ outcomes}}$$

An outcome is _____

An event is _____

The complement of an event is _____

_____

Examples

1 Finding Probability You select a letter at random from the letters F, G, H, and I. Find the probability of selecting a vowel. Express the probability as a fraction, a decimal, and a percent.

The event *vowel* has $\boxed{}$ outcome, $\boxed{}$, out of $\boxed{}$ possible outcomes.

$P(\text{vowel}) = \dfrac{\boxed{}}{\boxed{}}$ ← **number of favorable outcomes**

             ← **total number of possible outcomes**

$= \boxed{} = \boxed{}\%$ ← **Write as a decimal and percent.**

❷ Finding Probabilities from 0 to 1 A jar contains 1 blue marble, 3 green marbles, 3 yellow marbles, and 4 red marbles. You randomly select a marble from the jar. Find each probability.

a. P(red)

There are ☐ possible outcomes. Since there are ☐ red marbles, there are ☐ favorable outcomes.

P(red) $\dfrac{\boxed{}}{\boxed{}}$ ← **number of favorable outcomes**

← **total number of possible outcomes**

b. P(orange)

The event *orange* has ☐ favorable outcomes.

P(orange) $\dfrac{\boxed{}}{\boxed{}}$, or ☐   ← **number of favorable outcomes**

← **total number of possible outcomes**

c. P(not orange)

P(not orange) + P(orange) = ☐   ← **The sum of the probabilities of an even and its complement is 1.**

P(not orange) + ☐ = ☐   ← **Substitute** ☐ **for** *P*(orange).

P(not orange) = ☐   ← **Simplify.**

Quick Check

1. Find P(consonant) as a fraction for the letters A, B, C, D, and E.

☐

2. You roll a number cube once. Find each probability.

a. P(multiple of 3)

☐

b. P(not multiple of 2)

☐

c. P(9)

☐

Lesson 9-2

Experimental Probability

Lesson Objective	Common Core Standards
To find experimental probability and to use simulations	Statistics and Probability: 7.SP.6, 7.SP.7, 7.SP.7.b

Vocabulary and Key Concepts

Experimental Probability

$$P(\text{event}) = \frac{\text{number of times an event occurs}}{\text{total number of trials}}$$

Experimental probability is _____

_____

Examples

1 **Finding Experimental Probability** A manufacturer of computer parts checks 100 parts each day. On Monday, two of the checked parts are defective.

a. What is the experimental probability that a part is defective?

$P(\text{defective part}) = \dfrac{\boxed{}}{\boxed{}}$ ← number of defective parts
← total number of parts checked

$= \dfrac{\boxed{}}{\boxed{}}$ ← Simplify.

The experimental probability is $\dfrac{\boxed{}}{\boxed{}}$.

b. Which is the best prediction of the number of defective parts in Monday's total production of 1,250 parts?

A. 13 **B.** 25 **C.** 125 **D.** 250

Let x represent the predicted number of defective parts.

defective → $\dfrac{1}{\boxed{}} = \dfrac{x}{\boxed{}}$ ← defective
total → ← total ← Write a proportion.

$\boxed{} = x$ ← Solve the proportion.

You can predict $\boxed{}$ parts out of 1,250 parts to be defective. The correct answer is choice $\boxed{}$.

Daily Notetaking Guide

Name _____ Class _____ Date _____

❷ Simulating an Event A dog breeder knows that it is equally likely that a puppy will be male or female. Use a simulation to find the experimental probability that, in a litter of four puppies, all four will be male.

Simulate the problem by tossing four coins at the same time. Assume that male and female puppies are equally likely. Let "heads" represent a female and "tails" represent a male. A sample of 16 tosses is shown below.

Trial	Male	Female
1	//	//
2	/	///
3	////	
4	//	//
5	///	/
6	//	//
7	/	///
8	//	//

Trial	Male	Female
9	//	//
10	///	/
11	//	//
12	/	///
13	//	//
14		////
15	//	//
16	///	/

$P(\text{exactly four males}) = \dfrac{\boxed{}}{\boxed{}}$ ← number of times four tails occurs

← total number of trials

The experimental probability that, in a litter of four puppies, all four will be male is $\boxed{}$.

Quick Check

1. In 60 coin tosses, 25 are tails. Find the experimental probability.

2. The simulation uses coins to predict the genders of a family of three children, with "H" representing a girl and "T" representing a boy. What is the experimental probability that 3 children are all boys?

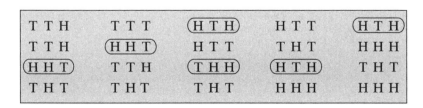

T T H	T T T	(H T H)	H T T	(H T H)
T T H	(H H T)	H T T	T H T	H H H
(H H T)	T T H	(T H H)	(H T H)	T H T
T H T	T H T	T H T	H H H	H H H

Lesson 9-3

Sample Spaces

Lesson Objective	Common Core Standards
To make and use sample spaces and to use the counting principle	Statistics and Probability: 7.SP.8, 7.SP.8.b

Vocabulary and Key Concepts

The Counting Principle

Suppose there are m ways of making one choice and n ways of making a second choice. There are $\boxed{} \times \boxed{}$ ways to make the first choice followed by the second choice.

Example If you can choose a shirt in 5 sizes and 7 colors, then you can choose $\boxed{} \times \boxed{}$, or $\boxed{}$, shirts.

A sample space is _____

_____

Example

❶ Finding a Sample Space

a. A spinner is divided into five equal sections labeled A–E. Make a table to show the sample space for spinning the spinner twice. Write the outcomes as ordered pairs.

$$\boxed{}$$

b. Find the probability of spinning at least one D.

There are $\boxed{}$ outcomes with at least one D. There are $\boxed{}$ possible outcomes. So, the probability of spinning at least one D is $\dfrac{\boxed{}}{\boxed{}}$.

Quick Check

1. Give the sample space for tossing two coins. Find the probability of getting two heads.

$\boxed{}$

Name _____ Class _____ Date _____

Examples

❷ Using a Tree Diagram Suppose you can go west or northwest by train, bus, or car.

a. Draw a tree diagram to show the sample space for your journey.

Train — West → Train, [____]

Train — Northwest → [____], Northwest

Bus — West → Bus, [____]

Bus — Northwest → [____], Northwest

← There are [____] possible outcomes.

Car — West → Car, [____]

Car — Northwest → [____], Northwest

b. What is the probability of a random selection that results in a bus trip west?

There is [_____] favorable outcome (bus, [_____]) out

of [_____] possible outcomes. The probability is [____].

❸ Using the Counting Principle How many kinds of coin purses are available if the purses come in small or large sizes and colors red, blue, yellow, and black?

Size	Colors
small	red
large	blue
	yellow
	black

Size
number of choices   ×   **Color**
number of choices

[____]   ×   [____]   =   [____]

There are [____] different kinds of coin purses available.

Quick Check

2. a. Suppose an airplane is added as another choice in Example 2.
Draw a tree diagram to show the sample space.

[ ]

b. Find the probability of selecting an airplane at random for your journey.

[_____]

3. A manager at the Deli Counter decides to add chicken to the list of meat choices. How many different sandwiches are now available?

[_____]

THE
DELI COUNTER
SANDWICHES

FRESH BREADS	DELI MEATS
Rye	Roast Beef
Wheat	Turkey
White	Ham
Pita	Pastrami
Wrap	Salami
	Liverwurst

Lesson 9-4

Compound Events

Lesson Objective	Common Core Standards
To find the probability of independent and dependent events	Statistics and Probability: 7.SP.8, 7.SP.8.a, 7.SP.8.b

Vocabulary and Key Concepts

Probability of Independent Events

If A and B are independent events,

then $P(A, \text{then } B) = $ [_____] $\times$ [_____] .

Probability of Dependent Events

If event B depends on event A, then

$P(A, \text{then } B) = $ [_____] $\times$ [_____] .

A compound event _____

Two events are independent if _____

_____

Two events are dependent if _____

_____

Examples

❶ Probability of Independent Events A spinner has equal sections labeled 1 to 10. Suppose you spin twice. Find $P(2, \text{then } 5)$.

A. $\frac{1}{10}$ **B.** $\frac{1}{5}$ **C.** $\frac{1}{40}$ **D.** $\frac{1}{100}$

The two events are independent. There are [____] possibilities on each spin.

$P(2, \text{then } 5) = P(2) \times$ [_____]   ← Spinning 2 is the first event.
                              Spinning 5 is the second event.

$= \frac{1}{10} \times \dfrac{\Box}{\Box} = \dfrac{\Box}{\Box}$ ← Substitute. Then multiply.

The probability that you will spin a 2 and then a 5 is [____]. The correct answer is choice [____].

❷ **Probability of Dependent Events** You select two cards at random from those with the letters on them as shown below. The two cards do not show vowels. Without replacing the two cards, you select a third card. Find the probability that you select a card with a vowel after you select the two cards without vowels.

P R O B A B I L I T Y

There are [   ] remaining after you select the first two cards.

P(vowel) = $\dfrac{\boxed{}}{\boxed{}}$ ← **number of remaining cards with vowels**
← **total number of remaining cards**

The probability of selecting a vowel for the third card is [   ].

❸ **Probability of Dependent Events** A bag contains 3 red marbles, 4 white marbles, and 1 blue marble. You draw one marble. Without replacing it, you draw a second marble. What is the probability that the two marbles you draw are red followed by white?

The two events are dependent. After the first selection, there are [   ] marbles to choose from.

P(red, then white) = P(red) × $\boxed{}$ ← **Use the formula for dependent events.**

$= \dfrac{3}{8} \times \dfrac{\boxed{}}{\boxed{}}$ ← **Substitute.**

$= \dfrac{\boxed{}}{\boxed{}} = \dfrac{\boxed{}}{\boxed{}}$ ← **Multiply. Then simplify.**

The probability that the two marbles are red and then white is [   ].

Quick Check

1. You and a friend play a game twice. Assume the probability of winning is $\dfrac{1}{2}$. Find P(win, then lose).

2. Use the cards in Example 2. You select a B card at random. Without replacing the B card, you select a second card. Find P(Y).

3. Suppose 52 cards, two each lettered A–Z, are put in a bucket. You select a card. Without replacing the first card, you select a second one. Find P(J, then J).

Lesson 9-5

Simulating Compound Events

Lesson Objective	Common Core Standard
To design and use simulations to estimate the probability of compound events	Statistics and Probability: 7.SP.8.c

Vocabulary

A simulation is _____

Each trial of a simulation _____

Examples

① Designing a Simulation A laundry company inserts a coupon for one free box of detergent inside $\frac{1}{5}$ of its detergent boxes. Design a simulation that can be used to estimate the probability that a customer will need to buy at least 3 boxes to get a coupon.

Step 1 Choose a simulation tool.

  $\frac{\boxed{}}{5}$ of the boxes include coupons, so use a tool that has $\boxed{}$ equally likely outcomes. A five-section spinner would be appropriate.

Step 2 Decide which outcomes are favorable.

  $\frac{\boxed{}}{5}$ of the outcomes should represent a box with a coupon. Let spinning a 1 represent a box with a coupon.

Step 3 Describe a trial.

  For each trial, spin until you get a $\boxed{}$. Keep track of the number of times you spin the spinner. This number represents the number of boxes the customer must buy to get a coupon for a free box.

② Using a Simulation to Estimate Probability Perform 20 trials of the simulation you designed in Example 1. Then estimate the probability that a customer will need to buy at least 3 boxes of detergent to get a coupon.

The table shows the results of 20 trials of the simulation. Of the 20 trials, $\boxed{}$ resulted in 3 or more boxes. So, the experimental probability that a customer will need to buy at least 3 boxes to get a coupon is approximately $\frac{\boxed{}}{\boxed{}}$, or $\frac{\boxed{}}{\boxed{}}$.

Boxes Needed to Get a Coupon	Frequency
1	IIII
2	I
3 or more	IIII IIII IIII

Name _____ Class _____ Date _____

❸ Using Random Digits as a Simulation Tool In an election, 43% of voters chose Governor Smith. Use random digits as a simulation tool to estimate the probability that a journalist will have to interview more than 2 voters before finding one who voted for Smith.

43% of voters, or $\dfrac{\boxed{}}{100}$, chose Smith.

Use a simulation tool with $\boxed{}$ equally likely outcomes. You can use 2-digit random numbers from 0 to 99. $\boxed{}$ of the possible outcomes should represent votes for Smith. Use the numbers 00 to 42.

Each row of random numbers represents one trial. If either or both numbers are between $\boxed{}$ and $\boxed{}$, the journalist will need to interview 1 or 2 voters.

If neither number is between 00 and $\boxed{}$, the journalist will need to interview more than 2 voters.

Out of 10 trials, $\boxed{}$ resulted in more than 2 voters being interviewed. So, the probability that a journalist will have to interview more than 2 voters before finding one who voted for Smith is approximately $\dfrac{\boxed{}}{10}$, or $\dfrac{\boxed{}}{\boxed{}}$.

Random Numbers		Outcome
02	85	← [ ] voters
70	13	← [ ] voters
97	56	← [ ] voters
32	24	← [ ] voters
60	58	← [ ] voters
41	30	← [ ] voters
29	12	← [ ] voters
62	83	← [ ] voters
54	78	← [ ] voters
20	18	← [ ] voters

Quick Check

1. One-fourth of the deer in a population has a certain disease. Design a simulation for estimating the probability that a scientist will need to test no more than 3 deer before finding one with the disease.

_____

_____

_____

_____

_____

2. Perform 20 trials of the simulation in Quick Check 1. Estimate the probability that a scientist will need to test no more than 3 deer before finding one that has the disease.

_____

3. Medicine In the U.S., 42% of blood donors have type A blood. Use the random numbers at the right as a tool to estimate the probability that it will take at least 4 donors to find one with type A blood.

Medicine			
91	04	81	49
72	45	45	96
54	93	14	81
70	28	66	00
67	37	29	45
33	77	57	22
58	84	14	80
49	45	20	59
78	05	88	88
21	83	16	98

A Note to the Student:

This section of your workbook contains a series of pages that support your mathematics understandings for each chapter and lesson presented in your student edition.

- Practice pages provide additional practice for every lesson.

- Guided Problem Solving pages lead you through a step-by-step solution to an application problem in each lesson.

- Vocabulary pages contain a variety of activities to increase your reading and math understanding, ranging from graphic organizers to vocabulary review puzzles.

Practice • Guided Problem Solving • Vocabulary

Name _____ Class _____ Date _____

Practice 1-1

Comparing and Ordering Integers

Name the integer represented by each point on the number line.

1. A _____   **2.** B _____   **3.** C _____   **4.** D _____   **5.** E _____   **6.** F _____

Compare. Use <, >, or =.

7. $-8 \;\square\; 8$ **8.** $4 \;\square\; -4$ **9.** $-5 \;\square\; 1$ **10.** $-8 \;\square\; 0$

11. $-6 \;\square\; -2$ **12.** $-1 \;\square\; -3$ **13.** $-4 \;\square\; 0$ **14.** $-3 \;\square\; 2$

Graph each integer and its opposite on the number line.

15. -9

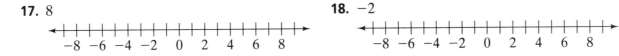

16. 5

17. 8

18. -2

Find the opposite of each number. You may find a number line helpful.

19. 2 **20.** -3 **21.** -38 **22.** $(-2 + 2)$

_____   _____   _____   _____

23. -44 **24.** $(5 + 2)$ **25.** -16 **26.** $(7 - 3)$

_____   _____   _____   _____

Write an integer to represent each situation.

27. a gain of 5 yards

_____

28. a debt of \$5

_____

29. a temperature of 100°F

_____

30. 135 feet below sea level

_____

1-1 • Guided Problem Solving

GPS **Student Page 7, Exercise 48:**

Sports In golf, the person with the lowest score is the winner. Rank the players below by ordering their scores from lowest to highest.

Player	Score
T. Woods	−12
V. Singh	−4
E. Els	+10
P. Mickelson	−3
R. Goosen	−5

Understand

1. Who wins in a golf game?

   _____

2. How will you determine the lowest number?

   _____

Plan and Carry Out

3. Draw a number line. Plot each score. Which number is the farthest to the left of zero on the number line?

   _____

4. What is the order of all five numbers? _____

5. Rank the players from lowest score to highest score.

   _____

   _____

Check

6. Is the person with the highest score last? Is the person with the lowest score first?

   _____

Solve Another Problem

7. Anne had the following golf scores this week: −6, +5, −4, +13, −2, +4, +6, −11. Which was her best score? Which was her worst score?

   _____

Practice 1-2

Adding and Subtracting Integers

Use a number line to find each sum.

1. $8 + (-4)$

2. $2 + (-3)$

3. $7 - 6$

_____   _____   _____

4. $(-4) + (-8)$

5. $3 + (-2)$

6. $15 + (-8)$

_____   _____   _____

Find each sum.

7. $-2 + (-3)$ **8.** $8 - 7 + 4$ **9.** $8 + (-5)$ **10.** $15 + (-3)$

_____   _____   _____   _____

11. $-16 + 8$ **12.** $7 + (-10)$ **13.** $-9 + (-5)$ **14.** $-12 + 14$

_____   _____   _____   _____

Find each difference.

15. $9 - 26$ **16.** $-4 - 15$ **17.** $21 - (-7)$ **18.** $27 - (-16)$

_____   _____   _____   _____

19. $-16 - (-43)$ **20.** $47 - 19$ **21.** $-156 - 98$ **22.** $-192 - 47$

_____   _____   _____   _____

23. $0 - (-51)$ **24.** $-63 - 89$ **25.** $-12 - (-21)$ **26.** $92 - (-16)$

_____   _____   _____   _____

Use >, <, or = to complete each statement.

27. $-9 - (-11)$ ☐ 0 **28.** $-17 + 20$ ☐ 0 **29.** $11 - (-4)$ ☐ 0

30. $28 - 19$ ☐ 0 **31.** $52 + (-65)$ ☐ 0 **32.** $-28 - (-28)$ ☐ 0

Solve.

33. The highest and lowest temperatures ever recorded in Africa are 136°F and −11°F. The highest temperature was recorded in Libya, and the lowest temperature was recorded in Morocco. What is the difference in these temperature extremes?

_____

34. The highest and lowest temperatures ever recorded in South America are 120°F and −27°F. Both the highest and lowest temperatures were recorded in Argentina. What is the difference in these temperature extremes?

_____

1-2 • Guided Problem Solving

GPS **Student Page 13, Exercise 27:**

Temperature The hottest temperature ever recorded in the United States was 134°F, measured at Death Valley, California. The coldest temperature, −80°F, was recorded at Prospect Creek, Alaska. What is the difference between these temperatures?

Understand

1. Circle the information you will need to solve the problem.

2. What are you being asked to do?

   _____

3. Which word tells you what operation to perform?

   _____

Plan and Carry Out

4. Write a subtraction expression for the problem.

   _____

5. Subtracting a negative number is the same as adding what type of number?

   _____

6. Write an addition expression that is the same as the expression you wrote in Step 4.

   _____

7. What is the difference between these temperatures?

   _____

Check

8. What is 134°F − 214°F?

   _____

Solve Another Problem

9. At 6:00 A.M. the temperature was 25°F. At 9:00 P.M. the temperature was −13°F. What was the difference in the temperature?

   _____

Practice 1-3

Complete each statement. Then write two examples to illustrate each relationship.

1. positive ÷ positive = ?

_____

2. negative · positive = ?

_____

3. positive · positive = ?

_____

4. negative ÷ negative = ?

_____

5. negative ÷ positive = ?

_____

6. positive · positive = ?

_____

7. positive ÷ negative = ?

_____

8. negative · negative = ?

_____

Estimate each product or quotient.

9. $-72 \cdot 57$

_____

10. $-92 \cdot (-41)$

_____

11. $-476 \div 90$

_____

12. $-83 \cdot 52$

_____

13. $538 \div (-63)$

_____

14. $-803 \cdot (-106)$

_____

15. $49 \cdot 61$

_____

16. $479 \div (-61)$

_____

Find each product or quotient.

17. $-\dfrac{36}{9}$

_____

18. $-\dfrac{52}{4}$

_____

19. $(-5) \cdot (-20)$

_____

20. $-\dfrac{63}{9}$

_____

21. $(-15) \cdot (2)$

_____

22. $-\dfrac{22}{2}$

_____

23. $(13) \cdot (-6)$

_____

24. $-\dfrac{100}{5}$

_____

25. $(-60) \cdot (-3)$

_____

26. $-\dfrac{240}{30}$

_____

27. $(43) \cdot (-8)$

_____

28. $-\dfrac{169}{13}$

_____

1-3 • Guided Problem Solving

GPS **Student Page 19, Exercise 35:**

Hobbies A scuba diver is 180 ft below sea level and rises to the surface at a rate of 30 ft/min. How long will the diver take to reach the surface?

Understand

1. Circle the information you will need to solve the problem.

2. What are you being asked to do?

   _____

   _____

Plan and Carry Out

3. Will you multiply or divide to solve this problem?

   _____

4. How far below sea level is the diver?

   _____

5. How fast is the diver rising?

   _____

6. How long will the diver take to reach the surface?

   _____

Check

7. What is 30 ft/min × 6 min? Does your answer equal the original distance below sea level?

   _____

Solve Another Problem

8. A rock climber climbs down into the Grand Canyon at a rate of 2 ft/min. How long will it take him to climb down 50 ft?

   _____

Name _____ Class _____ Date _____

Practice 1-4   Fractions and Decimals

Write each fraction as a decimal.

1. $\frac{3}{5}$ _____

2. $\frac{7}{8}$ _____

3. $\frac{7}{9}$ _____

4. $\frac{5}{16}$ _____

5. $\frac{1}{6}$ _____

6. $\frac{5}{8}$ _____

7. $\frac{1}{3}$ _____

8. $\frac{2}{3}$ _____

9. $\frac{9}{10}$ _____

10. $\frac{7}{11}$ _____

11. $\frac{9}{20}$ _____

12. $\frac{3}{4}$ _____

13. $\frac{4}{9}$ _____

14. $\frac{9}{11}$ _____

15. $\frac{11}{20}$ _____

Write each decimal as a mixed number or fraction in simplest form.

16. 0.6 _____

17. 0.45 _____

18. 0.62 _____

19. 0.8 _____

20. 0.325 _____

21. 0.725 _____

22. 4.75 _____

23. 0.33 _____

24. 0.925 _____

25. 3.8 _____

26. 4.7 _____

27. 0.05 _____

28. 0.65 _____

29. 0.855 _____

30. 0.104 _____

31. 0.47 _____

32. 0.894 _____

33. 0.276 _____

Order from least to greatest.

34. $0.\overline{2}, \frac{1}{5}, 0.02$

35. $1.\overline{1}, 1\frac{1}{10}, 1.101$

_____

_____

36. $\frac{6}{5}, 1\frac{5}{6}, 1.\overline{3}$

37. $4.\overline{3}, \frac{9}{2}, 4\frac{3}{7}$

_____

_____

38. A group of gymnasts were asked to name their favorite piece of equipment. 0.33 of the gymnasts chose the vault, $\frac{4}{9}$ chose the beam, and $\frac{1}{7}$ chose the uneven parallel bars. List their choices in order of preference from greatest to least.

_____

1-4 • Guided Problem Solving

Biology DNA content in a cell is measured in picograms (pg). A sea star cell has $\frac{17}{20}$ pg of DNA, a scallop cell has $\frac{19}{25}$ pg, a red water mite cell has 0.19 pg, and a mosquito cell has 0.024 pg. Order the DNA contents from greatest to least.

Understand

1. What are you being asked to do?

   _____

2. To order fractions and decimals, what must you do first?

   _____

   _____

Plan and Carry Out

3. Write the fraction $\frac{17}{20}$ as a decimal. _____

4. Write the fraction $\frac{19}{25}$ as a decimal. _____

5. Which organism has the smallest DNA content? _____

6. Which organism has the largest DNA content? _____

7. Order the DNA contents from greatest to least.

   _____

Check

8. Write 0.19 and 0.024 as fractions in simplest form. Order the DNA contents from greatest to least. Does your order check with that of Step 7?

   _____

   _____

Solve Another Problem

9. A solution calls for 0.25 oz of water, $\frac{2}{3}$ oz of vinegar, 0.6 oz of carbonate, and $\frac{9}{16}$ oz of lemon juice. Order the amounts from least to greatest.

   _____

Practice 1-5

Rational Numbers

Compare. Use <, >, or =.

1. $-\dfrac{2}{9} \, \square \, -\dfrac{4}{9}$

2. $-\dfrac{1}{6} \, \square \, -\dfrac{2}{3}$

3. $-\dfrac{5}{12} \, \square \, -\dfrac{3}{4}$

4. $-1.2 \, \square \, -2.1$

5. $-0.6 \, \square \, -0.52$

6. $-1.23 \, \square \, -1.25$

7. $-5.3 \, \square \, -5.\overline{3}$

8. $-3\dfrac{1}{4} \, \square \, -3.25$

9. $-4\dfrac{2}{5} \, \square \, -4.12$

Order from least to greatest.

10. $\dfrac{5}{4}, 1.5, -\dfrac{3}{2}, -0.5$

11. $\dfrac{1}{11}, -0.9, 0.069, \dfrac{1}{10}$

_____

12. $0.1\overline{2}, -\dfrac{11}{12}, -\dfrac{1}{6}, -0.1$

13. $\dfrac{2}{3}, 0.6, -\dfrac{5}{6}, -6.6$

_____

14. $1.312, 1\dfrac{3}{8}, -1\dfrac{3}{10}, -1.33$

15. $1, \dfrac{4}{5}, -\dfrac{8}{9}, -1$

_____

Evaluate. Write in simplest form.

16. $\dfrac{y}{z}$, for $y = -6$ and $z = -20$ _____

17. $\dfrac{2y}{-z}$, for $y = -5$ and $z = -12$ _____

18. $\dfrac{y + z}{2z}$, for $y = -4$ and $z = 8$ _____

19. $\dfrac{-2y + 1}{-z}$, for $y = 3$ and $z = 10$ _____

Compare.

20. The temperature at 3:00 A.M. was $-17.3°$F. By noon the temperature was $-17.8°$F. At what time was it the coldest?

_____

21. Samuel is $\dfrac{5}{8}$ in. taller than Jackie. Shelly is 0.7 in. taller than Jackie. Who is the tallest?

_____

1-5 • Guided Problem Solving

GPS **Student Page 29, Exercise 29:**

Animals About $\frac{1}{25}$ of a toad's eggs survive to adulthood. About 0.25 of a frog's eggs and $\frac{1}{5}$ of a green turtle's eggs survive to adulthood. Which animal's eggs have the highest survival rate?

Understand

1. Circle the information you will need to solve the problem.

2. What are you being asked to do?

   _____

   _____

3. In order to find the greatest number, what must you do first?

   _____

Plan and Carry Out

4. Write $\frac{1}{25}$ as a decimal. _____

5. Write $\frac{1}{5}$ as a decimal. _____

6. Which is the largest decimal,
   0.04, 0.2, or 0.25? _____

7. Which animal's eggs have
   the highest survival rate? _____

Check

8. What fraction is 0.25 equal to? Is it the greatest value?

   _____

Solve Another Problem

9. In order to organize the nails in a garage, Anne and Jeff measured the nails. Anne used fractions to measure her 3 groups of nails and found that they were $\frac{3}{5}$ in., $\frac{7}{12}$ in., and $\frac{4}{9}$ in. Jeff used decimals to measure his two groups and found that they were 0.62 in., and 0.31 in. Which nail is the longest?

   _____

Practice 1-6

Adding and Subtracting Rational Numbers

Find each sum.

1. $2.5 + (-7.9)$

2. $-2.92 + (-1.25)$

3. $-12.1 + 4.8$

4. $-\frac{3}{8} + \frac{1}{2}$

5. $-1\frac{1}{5} + \left(-\frac{1}{2}\right)$

6. $-6\frac{1}{8} + 1\frac{1}{4}$

7. $20\frac{5}{16} + \left(-12\frac{1}{4}\right)$

8. $-100.04 + (-4.01)$

9. $-8.33 + 7.17$

Find each difference.

10. $3.7 - (-12.4)$

11. $-5.55 - (-1.25)$

12. $-14.6 - 6.4$

13. $-\frac{5}{12} - \frac{1}{2}$

14. $2\frac{5}{8} - 2\frac{1}{4}$

15. $-4\frac{1}{4} - \left(-\frac{1}{2}\right)$

16. $90\frac{7}{16} - \left(-12\frac{1}{4}\right)$

17. $-5.04 - (-12.08)$

18. $-10.65 - 20.75$

19. What is the difference between -30.7 and -8.5?

20. The melting point of sodium is $208°F$. The melting point of mercury is $-37.7°F$. What is the difference in melting points of these two elements?

Name _____ Class _____ Date _____

1-6 • Guided Problem Solving ··

GPS **Student Page 35, Exercise 22:**

A diver climbs a 12 ft tower and walks $6\frac{3}{4}$ ft to the end of the diving board. Then he jumps $5\frac{1}{2}$ ft above the board and dives into the water. The water level is $1\frac{1}{4}$ ft below the base of the tower. How far does the diver travel from the top of the dive to the water?

Understand

1. Circle the information you will need to solve the problem.

2. What are you being asked to do?

   _____

   _____

3. What number is not needed to solve the problem? Explain.

   _____

   _____

Plan and Carry Out

4. What will you do first? _____

5. Do you need to rename any fractions or mixed numbers?

   _____

6. What is the sum of $5\frac{1}{2}$ and $1\frac{1}{4}$ _____

7. Will your final answer be negative or positive? Explain.

   _____

   _____

8. How far does the diver travel from the top of the dive to the

   water? _____

Check

9. How can you check your answer? _____

   _____

Solve Another Problem

10. Kirk began a carpentry project with $4\frac{1}{2}$ lb of nails. He gave $2\frac{1}{3}$ lb to his brother. Later he found he needed 3 lb of nails to finish the project. Write his shortage of nails as a signed number.

   _____

Name _____ Class _____ Date _____

Practice 1-7   **Multiplying Rational Numbers**

Find each product. Write your answers in simplest form.

1. $2\frac{3}{4} \cdot 1\frac{1}{2}$

2. $-\frac{3}{5} \cdot \frac{7}{9}$

3. $\left(1\frac{7}{8}\right)\left(-\frac{3}{5}\right)$

_____   _____   _____

4. $\left(-\frac{4}{5}\right)\left(-2\frac{3}{4}\right)$

5. $2\frac{1}{3} \cdot \left(-\frac{1}{5}\right)$

6. $\left(-4\frac{1}{3}\right)\left(\frac{5}{6}\right)$

_____   _____   _____

7. $\left(\frac{3}{8}\right)\left(2\frac{1}{9}\right)$

8. $-1\frac{1}{5} \cdot \left(\frac{1}{2}\right)$

9. $\left(1\frac{1}{4}\right)\left(1\frac{3}{4}\right)$

_____   _____   _____

Find each product.

10. $-1.3 \cdot (-4.8)$

11. $(12.5)\,(-0.2)$

12. $(4.9)(3.4)$

_____   _____   _____

13. $-3.7(5.4)$

14. $-6.5 \cdot (3.5)$

15. $(8.7)(-2.1)$

_____   _____   _____

16. $(-7.1)(-1.7)$

17. $9.3 \cdot (6.3)$

18. $(-10.06)(-6)$

_____   _____   _____

19. Maggie went on a hot air balloon ride. At its highest altitude, the balloon was at 1,500 feet, but Maggie's ride was at $\frac{1}{3}$ of that altitude most of the time. What was the altitude for most of Maggie's ride?

_____

20. An open parachute can descend $7\frac{3}{4}$ yards in one second. At that rate, what number represents the direction and distance it descends in 6 seconds?

_____

1-7 • Guided Problem Solving

GPS **Student Page 41, Exercise 27:**

Mental Math Richard's cell phone bill is $29.99 a month. Each month this amount is automatically taken from his checking account. In 6 months, what is the change to his checking account for his cell phone bills?

Understand

1. What information are you given? _____

2. What are you being asked to do? _____

_____

3. What number represents the amount automatically taken from the checking account each month? _____

Plan and Carry Out

4. How can you estimate the answer? _____

_____

5. What operation will you use to find the change to his checking account? _____

6. Will the answer be positive or negative number? Explain.

_____

7. What is the change to his checking account for his cell phone bills? _____

Check

8. Explain how you can use mental math to check your answer.

_____

_____

9. Does your answer check?

_____

Solve Another Problem

10. You have $10\frac{1}{2}$ pounds of flour in a bin. If you use $\frac{1}{2}$ pound of flour in each of 6 recipes, what will be the amount of flour remaining in the bin?

_____

Practice 1-8

Find each quotient. Write your answers in simplest form.

1. $-4\frac{1}{2} \div \frac{1}{4}$

2. $1\frac{9}{10} \div \left(-\frac{5}{8}\right)$

3. $1\frac{1}{8} \div 2\frac{1}{2}$

4. $6\frac{1}{3} \div \frac{2}{3}$

5. $\left(-\frac{3}{5}\right) \div \left(-1\frac{1}{3}\right)$

6. $\frac{9}{10} \div \left(-\frac{3}{4}\right)$

7. $\left(-\frac{5}{8}\right) \div \left(-\frac{3}{4}\right)$

8. $-3\frac{1}{4} \div 1\frac{1}{2}$

9. $\left(-2\frac{1}{5}\right) \div 10$

Find each quotient.

10. $-73.1 \div 4.3$

11. $2.73 \div (-0.7)$

12. $(-8.75) \div (-2.5)$

13. $4.44 \div (-3.7)$

14. $0.072 \div 0.08$

15. $-76.44 \div 9.1$

16. $(-0.115) \div (-0.23)$

17. $5.94 \div -11$

18. $(-0.802) \div (-4.01)$

19. Zain owes $1,312.50 for a new computer. An equal amount will be taken from his bank account each month for $10\frac{1}{2}$ months. How much will be taken out each month?

20. A marine biologist is measuring the temperature of a lake at 6 equally spaced depths. She makes her measurements at a point where the lake is 33.6 feet deep. What signed number represents the distance and direction of the first measurement from the lake's surface?

1-8 • Guided Problem Solving

GPS **Student Page 46, Exercise 25:**

Lucille had 48 oz of dried blueberries. Each batch of muffins uses 3.6 oz of dried blueberries. After making several batches, 30 oz of the dried blueberries are left. How many batches of muffins did she make?

Understand

1. What information are you given? _____

   _____

2. What are you being asked to do?

   _____

3. How many steps must you do to solve the problem? _____

Plan and Carry Out

4. What operation(s) will you use to solve the problem?

   _____

5. How many ounces of blueberries did Lucille use for the batches she made? _____

6. How will you find the number of batches Lucille made?

   _____

7. How many batches of muffins did she make? _____

Check

8. How can you check your answer? _____

   _____

   _____

9. Does your answer check? _____

Solve Another Problem

10. Charlie made apple-walnut cakes. He had 40 oz of walnuts and used $6\frac{1}{2}$ ounces for each cake. If he has 14 oz walnuts left, how many cakes did he bake?

    _____

1A: Graphic Organizer

Study Skill As you begin a new textbook, look through the table of contents to see what kind of information you will be learning during the year. Notice that some of the topics were introduced last year. Get a head start by reviewing your old notes and problems.

Write your answers.

1. What is the chapter title? _____

2. How many lessons are there in this chapter? _____

3. What is the topic of the Test-Taking Strategies page? _____

4. Complete the graphic organizer below as you work through the chapter.
   - In the center, write the title of the chapter.
   - When you begin a lesson, write the lesson name in a rectangle.
   - When you complete a lesson, write a skill or key concept in a circle linked to that lesson block.
   - When you complete the chapter, use this graphic organizer to help you review.

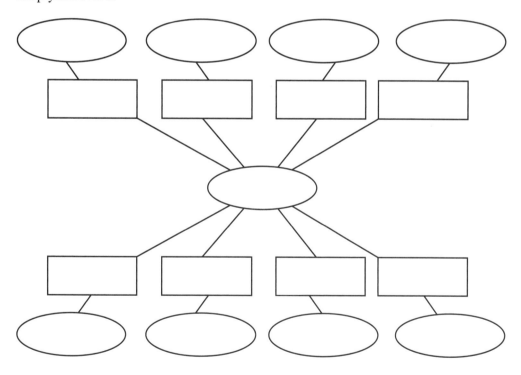

1B: Reading Comprehension

For use after Lesson 1-5

Study Skill Practice reading charts and tables in books, magazines, or newspapers since information is often organized this way.

The table below contains information about four of the highest-ranked centers in the history of the National Basketball Association (NBA).

Use the table below to answer the questions.

Player	Height, Weight	Number of Seasons to Playoffs	Points Per Game (PPG) During Regular Season	PPG During Playoffs	NBA Titles	Age at Retirement
Kareem Abdul-Jabbar	7 ft 2 in. 267 lb	20 to 18	24.6	24.3	6	42
Wilt Chamberlain	7 ft 1 in. 275 lb	14 to 13	30.1	22.5	2	37
Shaquille O'Neal	7 ft 1 in. 325 lb	19 to 17	23.7	24.3	4	39
Bill Russell	6 ft 10 in. 220 lb	13 to 13	15.1	16.2	11	35

1. Which of these centers is the tallest? _____

2. Which center is the shortest? _____

3. Which center won the most NBA titles? _____

4. Which center weighed the greatest amount? _____

5. Which center played the most regular seasons? _____

6. Which center(s) played in the playoffs 13 times?

   _____

7. What does PPG stand for? _____

8. Which center had the highest PPG during the regular season?

   _____

9. **High-Use Academic Words** In the directions, you are told that the NBA centers in the table are *ranked* the highest. What does it mean to *rank*?

   a. to show clearly   **b.** to determine the relative position of

1C: Reading/Writing Math Symbols

For use after Lesson 1-6

Study Skill Finish one homework assignment before beginning another. Sometimes it helps to start with the most difficult assignment first.

Match the symbol in Column A with its meaning in Column B.

Column A	Column B
1. ·	**A.** division
2. >	**B.** degrees
3. ÷	**C.** is greater than
4. ‖	**D.** multiplication
5. °	**E.** is less than
6. <	**F.** absolute value

Each of the following expressions uses a bar symbol in a different way. Explain the meaning of the bar in each expression.

7. $\dfrac{8}{11}$ _____

8. -6.5 _____

9. $0.\overline{35}$ _____

10. $14 - 9$ _____

1D: Visual Vocabulary Practice

For use after Lesson 1-7

Study Skill If a word is not in the glossary, use a dictionary to find its meaning.

Concept List

absolute value	opposites
additive inverses	rational numbers
Commutative Property of Addition	repeating decimals
Distributive Property	terminating decimals
integers	

Write the concept that best describes each exercise. Choose from the concept list above.

1. $\frac{4}{7}, 3.4, -2, 6\,\frac{1}{3}$	2. $-17, 0, 8$	3. $\begin{aligned}|-6| &= 6 \\ |6| &= 6\end{aligned}$
4. $\begin{aligned}|-6| + -6 &= 0 \\ 7.5 + (-7.5) &= 0\end{aligned}$	5. $\begin{aligned}&26.387 \\ &41.0 \\ &306.904\end{aligned}$	6. $8(2^3 + 16) = 8(2^3) + 8(16)$
7. $b + c = c + b$	8. $\begin{aligned}&-12 \text{ and } 12 \\ &-9.6 \text{ and } 9.6 \\ &-40 \text{ and } 40\end{aligned}$	9. $\begin{aligned}43.\overline{7} &= 43.77\ldots \\ 2.\overline{18} &= 2.181818\ldots \\ 1.\overline{302} &= 601.302302302\ldots\end{aligned}$

1E: Vocabulary Check

Study Skill Strengthen your vocabulary. Use these pages and add cues and summaries by applying the Cornell Notetaking style.

Write the definition for each word or term at the right. To check your work, fold the paper back along the dotted line to see the correct answers.

_____

_____

_____   absolute value

_____

_____   integers

_____

_____   repeating decimal

_____

_____   rational number

_____

_____   additive inverses

_____

_____

Vocabulary and Study Skills

1E: Vocabulary Check (continued)

Write the vocabulary word or term for each definition. To check your work, fold the paper forward along the dotted line to see the correct answers.

the distance of a number from
0 on the number line

_____

the set of positive whole numbers,
their opposites, and 0

_____

a decimal with one or more digits
that repeat without end

_____

a number that can be written
as a quotient of two integers,
where the divisor is not 0

_____

any two numbers whose
sum is 0

_____

1F: Vocabulary Review Puzzle

For use with the Chapter Review

Study Skill Vocabulary is an important part of every subject you learn. Review new words and their definitions using flashcards.

Find each of the following words in the word search. Circle the word and then cross it off the word list. Words can be displayed forwards, backwards, up, down, or diagonally.

absolute	integers	ordering
decimal	inverses	repeating
opposites	rational	commutative
terminating	distributive	multiplication

```
O E E U L A V E T U L O S B A
D Y D C G A A Q V E N S R O N
R W I U L T I P L I V E P I O
E X S K R L A N R V P F T L I
R A T I O N A L M E Q L E R T
T N R S U R E A D V I R J A
I J I Q E V I T A T U M M O C
O N B Z S T I F K R S R I R I
N L U E K N I P M R H Z N D L
L M T U G D V S E N N V A E P
B N I X U G M G O H X R T R I
I N V E R S E S S P H F I I T
C V E S M T S N H K P P N N L
M B R C N N F R C S P O G G U
D E C I M A L X R Z O A P D M
```

Name _____ Class _____ Date _____

Practice 2-1 .... Evaluating and Writing Algebraic Expressions

Evaluate each expression using the values $m = 7$, $r = 8$, and $t = 2$.

1. $5m - 6$

_____

2. $4m + t$

_____

3. $r \div t$

_____

4. $m \times t$

_____

5. $5t + 2m$

_____

6. $r \times m$

_____

7. $3m - 5t$

_____

8. $(m \times r) \div t$

_____

9. mrt

_____

10. Write an algebraic expression for the nth term of the table below.

A	0	1	2	3	4	5	n
B	3	5	7	9	11	13	?

_____

Write a word phrase for each algebraic expression.

11. $n + 16$

_____

12. $3.2n$

_____

13. $25.6 - n$

_____

14. $n \div 24$

_____

15. $\dfrac{45}{n}$

_____

16. $15.4 - n$

_____

Write an algebraic expression for each word phrase.

17. 12 more than m machines

_____

18. six times the daily amount of fiber f in your diet

_____

19. your aunt's age a minus 25

_____

20. the total number of seashells s divided by 10

_____

21. You and four friends plan a surprise party. Each of you contributes the same amount of money m for food.

   a. Write an algebraic expression for the total amount of money contributed for food. _____

   b. Evaluate your expression for $m = \$5.25$. _____

2-1 • Guided Problem Solving

GPS **Student Page 60, Exercise 38:**

```
6-4462   Daalling V 8 Everett All.........
2-3302   ........................ly R.......
4-1775   Dabady V 94 Burns de All.....
2-0014   Dabagh L 13 Lanca ter R.......
6-3356   Dabagh W Dr 521 V eston All..
4-7322   Dabar G 98 River A ...........
6-1530   Dabarera F 34 Ros and All....
2-2279   Dabas M 17 Rivers e R.......
4-9978   D'Abate D 86 Moss ill Rd All.
2-6745   D'Abate G 111 Sou Central R
4-5456   Dabbous H 670 Wa ren Dr All..
6-3064   Dabbraccio F 151 entury All..
6-2257   Dabby D 542 Waln All........
2-9987   ....................Green R....
6-5643   Dabcovich M 72 Main All.......
```

Estimation This section of a page from a telephone directory shows a column with 11 names in 1 inch. Each page has four 10-inch columns. Write an algebraic expression for the approximate number of names in p pages of the directory.

Understand

1. What are you being asked to do?

   _____

   _____

2. What is an algebraic expression?

   _____

   _____

3. What does p represent?

   _____

   _____

Plan and Carry Out

4. How many names are in 1 in. of one column? _____

5. How many names are in one 10-in. column? _____

6. How many names are in four 10-in. columns? _____

7. How many names are listed on one page? _____

8. How many names are listed on p pages? _____

9. Write an algebraic expression for the approximate number of names in p pages of the directory. _____

Check

10. Substitute $p = 1, 2,$ and 3 in the expression and solve. Does your expression provide reasonable values?

    _____

Solve Another Problem

11. The yearbook committee can fit 1 student picture in one inch of a row. If there are eight 6-inch rows on each page, write an expression for the approximate number of pictures that can fit on p pages.

    _____

Practice 2-2

Simplifying Expressions

Simplify each expression.

1. $12 - \frac{2}{3}m + 4 - \frac{3}{4}m$

2. $a - 2 + 13 + 8a$

3. $10q - 2q + 3 - 9$

4. $8 - g - 2 + 5g$

5. $2.2k + 5 + 7.9k + 8$

6. $-4r - 2r - 6 - 4$

7. $0.2(15 - 3t) - 1.8$

8. $7x - 5(3x + 12)$

9. $\frac{1}{3}(9z - 27) + 12$

Factor each expression completely.

10. $42r - 18$

11. $100 - 50d$

12. $24x + 64$

13. $-9y - 39$

14. $60 - 24x$

15. $9w - 81$

16. $132 + 77t$

17. $16y - 56$

Use >, <, or = to make each statement true.

18. $-4 + p + 2$ ⬤ $4p + 2 \cdot 4 - 3p$ _____

19. $2m + 2n - 5$ ⬤ $6 + 2(m + n) - 11$ _____

20. $3x + 4 - 4x + 2$ ⬤ $3(5 - x) + 2x$ _____

21. Find the perimeter of a rectangle with length $3c - 5$ and width $2c$. Simplify your answer.

2-2 • Guided Problem Solving

GPS **Student Page 65, Exercise 39:**

Earning Money You work 40 hours a week and earn d dollars an hour. You get a raise of $3 an hour plus a $13 bonus in the first week. Write and simplify the expression that shows the amount you will earn in the week.

Understand

1. What are you being asked to do?

   _____

   _____

2. What does it mean to simplify an expression?

   _____

   _____

3. What does d stand for?

   _____

   _____

Plan and Carry Out

4. At first, how much do you earn an hour? _____

5. How much do you earn an hour after your raise? _____

6. How many hours do you work in a week? _____

7. Write an expression to show how much you earn a week. _____

8. How much was your bonus? _____

9. How much did you earn the first week? Write and simplify the expression.

   _____

Check

10. Substitute $d = 5$ in the expression. Does your expression seem reasonable?

    _____

Solve Another Problem

11. You make 40 shirts a week and earn p dollars per shirt. You get a raise of $1.50 a shirt plus a $22 bonus in the first week. Write and simplify the expression that shows the amount you will earn in the week.

    _____

Practice 2-3

Solving One-Step Equations

Solve each equation. Check your answer.

1. $n + 2 = 5$

2. $x - 1 = -3$

3. $7 = a + 2$

4. $p + 2 = -6$

_____

_____

_____

_____

5. $-18 = -\dfrac{y}{2}$

6. $\dfrac{y}{16} = 3$

7. $-56 = 8r$

8. $9w = -63$

_____

_____

_____

_____

Use a calculator, paper and pencil, or mental math. Solve each equation.

9. $-3v = -48$

10. $13 = -\dfrac{x}{4}$

11. $28 = -4a$

12. $-\dfrac{t}{42} = 3$

_____

_____

_____

_____

13. $t + 43 = 28$

14. $-19 = r + 6$

15. $25 = r + 7$

16. $13 = 24 + c$

_____

_____

_____

_____

Write and solve an equation to represent each situation.

17. The odometer on your family car reads 20,186.7 after going 62.3 miles. How many miles were on the odometer before going 62.3 miles?

_____

18. Michael bought a $25.00 gift for a friend. After he bought the gift, Michael had $176.89. Write and solve an equation to calculate how much money Michael had before he bought the gift.

_____

19. This spring it rained a total of 11.5 inches. This was 3 inches less than last spring. Write and solve an equation to find the amount of rain last season.

_____

20. One of the largest flowers, the Rafflesia, weighs about 15 lb. How many Rafflesia flowers can be placed in a container that can hold a maximum of 240 lb?

_____

21. "Heavy water" is a name given to a compound used in some nuclear reactors. Heavy water costs about $1,500 per gallon. If a nuclear plant spent $10,500 on heavy water, how many gallons of heavy water were bought?

_____

2-3 • Guided Problem Solving

GPS Student Page 71, Exercise 22:

Biology A student collects 12 ladybugs for a science project. This is 9 fewer than the number of ladybugs the student collected yesterday. Write and solve an equation to find the number of ladybugs the student collected yesterday.

Understand

1. Circle the information you will need to solve the problem.

2. What are you being asked to do?

   _____

   _____

3. What will your variable represent?

   _____

   _____

Plan and Carry Out

4. How many ladybugs did the student
   collect today?   _____

5. Determine a variable for the number
   of ladybugs the student collected yesterday. _____

6. Write an expression for the phrase;
   *9 fewer than the number of ladybugs
   the student collected yesterday.*   _____

7. Write an equation that compares the answer
   to step 4 with the answer to Step 6.   _____

8. Solve the equation written in Step 7. _____

9. How many ladybugs did the student
   collect yesterday?   _____

Check

10. Substitute the answer to Step 9 into the equation for the variable and solve.

    _____

Solve Another Problem

11. Jason is 72 in. tall. If Kenny is 15 in. shorter than Jason, write and solve an equation for the height of Kenny.

    _____

Guided Problem Solving

Practice 2-4

Exploring Two-Step Equations

Define a variable and write an algebraic expression for each phrase.

1. six times the price of gas minus 20

_____

2. one-half the distance from Boston to New York minus 25

_____

3. two fewer than five times the number of eggs needed in the recipe

_____

4. 10 megabytes less than the number of megabytes in a computer, divided by 6

_____

Solve each equation using number sense.

5. $10 + 5h = 25$

_____

6. $8s - 8 = 64$

_____

7. $3y + 78 = 81$

_____

8. $2g + 4 = 12$

_____

9. $5j + 5 = 15$

_____

10. $3w + 8 = 20$

_____

11. $\frac{h}{2} + 1 = 4$

_____

12. $\frac{g}{g} + 12 = 16$

_____

13. $2 + \frac{b}{7} = 3$

_____

14. For a walk-a-thon a sponsor committed to give you a flat fee of $5 plus $2 for every mile you walk. Write an expression for the total amount you will collect from your sponsor at the end of the walk-a-thon. Then evaluate your expression for 20 miles walked.

_____

2-4 • Guided Problem Solving

GPS **Student Page 78, Exercise 39:**

Food You are helping to prepare food for a large family gathering. You can slice 2 zucchinis per minute. You need 30 sliced zucchinis. How long will it take you to finish, if you have already sliced 12 zucchinis?

Understand

1. Circle the information you will need to solve the problem.

2. What are you being asked to do?

   _____

   _____

3. What will your variable represent?

   _____

Plan and Carry Out

4. How many sliced zucchinis do you need?   _____

5. How many sliced zucchinis do you
   already have?   _____

6. Write and simplify an expression for the
   number of zucchinis you still need to slice.   _____

7. To calculate the number of minutes it will take
   to slice the remaining zucchinis, what number
   will you divide your answer to Step 7 by?   _____

8. Write an equation to solve the problem.   _____

9. How long will it take you to finish slicing
   the remaining zucchinis?   _____

Check

10. Multiply your answer to Step 9 by your answer to Step 7. Does your answer match your result from Step 6?

    _____

Solve Another Problem

11. Jordan skates 6 mi/h. Today she has already skated 8 miles. Her goal is to skate a total of 20 miles. How much longer does she have to skate to reach her goal?

    _____

Guided Problem Solving

Practice 2-5

Solving Two-Step Equations

Solve each equation. Then check your answer.

1. $7m + 8 = 71$

2. $\frac{y}{7} + 6 = 11$

3. $12y + 2 = 146$

4. $\frac{m}{9} - 17 = 21$

_____

_____

_____

_____

5. $\frac{y}{-12} + 1 = 6$

6. $2a - 1 = 19$

7. $\frac{c}{9} - 8 = 17$

8. $-4t + 16 = 24$

_____

_____

_____

_____

9. $\frac{b}{-2} - 8 = -6$

10. $3d + 14 = 11$

11. $\frac{z}{17} - 1 = 8$

12. $\frac{e}{5} - 14 = 21$

_____

_____

_____

_____

13. $\frac{f}{-9} + 4 = 2$

14. $-2y + 16 = 10$

15. $4w - 26 = 82$

16. $\frac{j}{19} - 2 = -5$

_____

_____

_____

_____

Solve each equation.

17. $3n - 8 = 4$

18. $\frac{n}{5} - 4 = 11$

_____

_____

19. $2n - 3 = 9$

20. $1 + \frac{n}{4} = 9$

_____

_____

Match each sentence with a two-step equation.

21. Half of the height of a tree minus five equals fifteen.

_____

22. Two less than three times the number of feet of fencing required equals twelve feet.

_____

A. $3n - 2 = 12$

B. $3n + 2 = 12$

C. $\frac{n}{2} - 5 = 15$

D. $\frac{n}{4} - 8 = -5$

23. Eight less than the quotient of Dave's golf score and four equals negative five.

_____

24. Three times Gail's age increased by two years equals twelve years.

_____

2-5 • Guided Problem Solving

GPS **Student Page 83, Exercise 32:**

Jobs You earn $20 per hour landscaping a yard. You pay $1.50 in bus fare each way. How many hours must you work to earn $117?

Understand

1. Circle the information you will need to solve the problem.

2. What are you being asked to do?

   _____

   _____

3. How much do you spend in bus fare
   to go to and from work?   _____

Plan and Carry Out

4. Write an expression for the amount of money you make after
   h hours.

   _____

5. Write an expression for the amount of money you have after you
   pay for bus fare.

   _____

6. How much money do you need to earn? _____

7. Write an equation that can be solved for *h*. _____

8. Solve the equation. _____

9. How many hours must you work to earn $117? _____

Check

10. Substitute the answer in Step 9 into the equation for the variable
    and solve.

    _____

Solve Another Problem

11. You charge $6 per hour to babysit one child. You charge an
    additional $2 per hour for each additional child. The Taylors have
    4 children. How many hours would you have to babysit the
    Taylors' children to earn $84?

    _____

Practice 2-6

Solving Equations Involving the Distributive Property

Solve each equation.

1. $-4(h + 8) = 24$

2. $5(b + 12) = 65$

3. $12\left(p - 2\frac{1}{3}\right) = -8$

4. $0.8(2 - g) = 3.2$

5. $2.6(m + 1.9) = 6.5$

6. $1\frac{1}{2}\left(n - 4\frac{1}{2}\right) = 12$

7. $-2\left(t + 4\frac{2}{3}\right) = 9\frac{1}{2}$

8. $2.4(x + 4) = 21.9$

9. $-7(y - 12) = -147$

10. $-1(d + 5) = 11.4$

11. $-3(z - 8) = 22$

12. $0.2(f + 15) = 3$

13. $4(s + 7) = 84$

14. $3.2(w - 6.5) = 28.8$

15. $-7(5.8 + q) = -84$

16. Each classroom kit contains supplies for 27 students. In it, there are spinners and 5 number cubes per student. If there are 189 items in the kit, how many spinners are there per student?

_____

17. Ken makes a salad for 20 people. The salad dressing contains olive oil and $\frac{1}{8}$ cup lemon juice per person. If there are $3\frac{3}{4}$ cups of dressing, how many cups of olive oil did Ken add per person?

_____

2-6 • Guided Problem Solving

GPS **Student Page 92, Exercise 23:**

Cell Phone Paulo pays $45.99 per month for unlimited calls, with additional charges for text messages. His bill for 4 months is $207.96. If he sends 100 texts each month, how much is he charged per text?

Understand

1. What are you being asked to do?

   _____

   _____

2. What are you going to use to solve the problem?

   _____

   _____

3. What variable will you use and what will it stand for?

   _____

Plan and Carry Out

4. What is Paulo charged per month, with no text messages? _____

5. Write an expression to show how much he is charged for 4 months. _____

6. What is he charged for 100 text messages? _____

7. Write an expression to show how much he is charged for 4 months with text messages. _____

8. What is his bill for 4 months? _____

9. Write an equation to solve the problem. _____

10. How much is he charged for each text? _____

Check

11. Substitute the cost of a text in the equation. Does it make a true equation?

   _____

Solve Another Problem

12. George rides a cab to work 3 days a week. He pays $3.50 for the cab to pick him up. He pays an additional fee for each mile driven. In one week, George paid $35.25. If he rides 11 miles each day, how much does he pay per mile?

   _____

2A: Graphic Organizer

For use before Lesson 2-1

Study Skill Develop consistent study habits. Block off the same amount of time each evening for schoolwork. Plan ahead by setting aside extra time when you have a big project or test coming up.

Write your answers.

1. What is the chapter title? _____

2. How many lessons are there in this chapter? _____

3. What is the topic of the Test-Taking Strategies page? _____

4. Complete the graphic organizer below as you work through the chapter.
   - In the center, write the title of the chapter.
   - When you begin a lesson, write the lesson name in a rectangle.
   - When you complete a lesson, write a skill or key concept in a circle linked to that lesson block.
   - When you complete the chapter, use this graphic organizer to help you review.

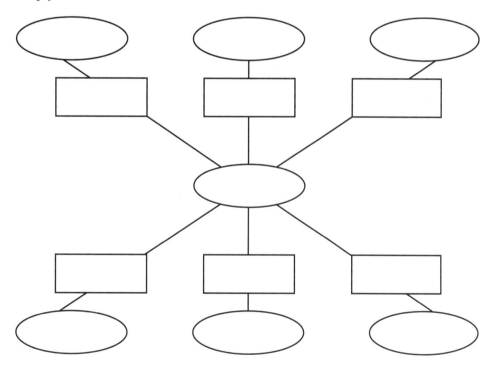

2B: Reading Comprehension

For use after Lesson 2-5

Study Skill Never go to class unprepared. List your assignments, books needed, and supplies to help you prepare.

Read the paragraph and answer the questions.

Old Faithful is the most famous geyser at Yellowstone National Park. It erupts approximately every $1\frac{1}{4}$ hours for up to 5 minutes. When it erupts, a mixture of water and steam shoots into the air as high as 170 feet. The amount of water expelled during each eruption ranges from 10,000 to 12,000 gallons. Giant Geyser and Steamboat Geyser, two other geysers at Yellowstone, shoot water to heights of 200 feet and 380 feet, respectively.

1. What is the paragraph about?

   _____

2. Which number in the paragraph is written as a mixed number?

   _____

3. For what fraction of an hour does Old Faithful erupt?

   _____

4. Which of the geysers shoots water to the greatest height when it erupts?

   _____

5. What is the rate, in gallons per minute, of Old Faithful's eruptions?

   _____

   _____

6. **High-Use Academic Words** In the study skill given at the top of the page, what does it mean to *list*?

   a. to enumerate   **b.** to locate on a map

2C: Reading/Writing Math Symbols .... For use after Lesson 2-1

Study Skill Mathematics builds on itself, so build a strong foundation.

Match each expression with its word form.

1. $x - 3$ **A.** six more than a number

2. $4m$ **B.** the quotient of a number and five

3. $\dfrac{7}{x}$ **C.** a number decreased by three

4. $m + 6$ **D.** seven divided by a number

5. $m \div 5$ **E.** four multiplied by a number

Write a mathematical expression or equation for each word description.

6. nine less than the product of eleven and x

_____

7. a number plus four equals thirteen

_____

8. the quotient of x and 4

_____

9. the absolute value of a number

_____

Write two different word phrases for each of the following expressions.

10. $x - 10$

_____

_____

11. $5m$

_____

_____

12. $-8 + p$

_____

_____

2D: Visual Vocabulary Practice

Study Skill Making sense of mathematical symbols is like reading a foreign language that uses different letters.

Concept List

Addition Property of Equality	Subtraction Property of Equality
Division Property of Equality	Multiplication Property of Equality
variable	inverse operations
algebraic expression	like terms
coefficient	

Write the concept that best describes each exercise. Choose from the concept list above.

1. If $5 - y = 2 - 3y$, then $5 - y + 3y = 2 - 3y + 3y$. _____	**2.** $t + 8$ $7r$ $3 - y$ _____	**3.** $16n$ and $3n$ are; $18p$ and $27r$ are not _____
4. z in the equation $\frac{2z}{5} = 12$ _____	**5.** If $6 + w = 9w$, then $6 + w - w = 9w - w$. _____	**6.** 4 in the equation $4x = 12$ _____
7. If $5b = 3$, then $\frac{5b}{5} = \frac{3}{5}$. _____	**8.** addition and subtraction represent this in $7x + 12 = 183$ $7x + 12 - 12 = 183$ _____	**9.** If $3t \div 9 = 32$, then $3t \div 9 \cdot 9 = 32 \cdot 9$. _____

2E: Vocabulary Check

For use after Lesson 2-3

Study Skill Strengthen your vocabulary. Use these pages and add cues and summaries by applying the Cornell Notetaking style.

Write the definition for each word or term at the right. To check your work, fold the paper back along the dotted line to see the correct answers.

_____   variable

_____

_____

_____   algebraic expression

_____

_____

_____   like terms

_____

_____

_____   coefficient

_____

_____

_____   inverse operations

_____

_____

Vocabulary and Study Skills

2E: Vocabulary Check (continued)

Write the vocabulary word or term for each definition. To check your work, fold the paper forward along the dotted line to see the correct answers.

a symbol that represents one or more numbers

_____

a mathematical expression with at least one variable

_____

terms that have the same variable factors

_____

a numerical factor of a term with a variable

_____

operations that undo each other

_____

2F: Vocabulary Review Puzzle

For use with the Chapter Review

Vocabulary and Study Skills

Study Skill Use a notebook or a section of a loose-leaf binder for math assignments. Review problems that gave you trouble.

Unscramble each of the key words from the chapter to help you fill in the famous quote by Walt Disney. Match the letters in the numbered cells with the numbered cells at the bottom.

ABRUCSTNOIT EPYPRORT [ ][ ][ ][C][ ][ ][ ] [ ][ ][ ][ ][T][ ]
                      17   22   13   5

FO QUIETALY [ ][ ] [Q][ ][ ][ ][ ]
             20   39 28   16

VENISER AEPRSOONTI [I][ ][ ][ ] [ ][ ][ ][O][ ][ ]
                      21   37   32   25   10

LAGIACRBE REEXSONSIP [ ][ ][ ][ ][I][ ] [ ][ ][ ][ ][O]
                       30   31   11   26   36   12

BIVEALRA [ ][ ][ ][L][ ]
          23 7 1   41

TDINAIOD TEPPYORR [ ][ ][ ][O][ ] [ ][ ][ ][R][ ]
                    9   33   29   15

  FO TIELYQAU [ ][ ] [ ][ ][L][ ]
               27   4   40

IICEOEFTNCF [ ][ ][F][ ][ ][ ]
             3   24

EILK ERSMT [ ][K] [T][ ][ ]
            19   14

IDNOSIIV ERPYROPT [ ][ ][S][ ][ ] [ ][ ][ ][R][ ]
                    6   34   35   8

  FO EUIYQTAL [ ][ ] [ ][ ][A][ ]
               18 38   2

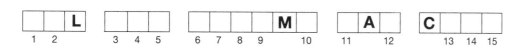

[ ][L] [ ][ ][ ] [ ][ ][ ][M][ ] [ ][A] [C][ ][ ]
1 2   3 4 5   6 7 8   10   11   12   13 14 15

[R][ ][ ] [ ][ ] [W][ ] [H][ ][ ] [ ][H]
16   18 19 20   21   22 23 24   25 26

[C][ ][ ][ ][ ][ ] [ ][ ] [U][ ][ ][ ] [ ][H][M] .
27 28 29 30 31 32   33 34   35 36 37 38 39 40   41

Name _____ Class _____ Date _____

Practice 3-1

Graphing and Writing Inequalities

Graph the solution of each inequality on a number line.

1. $x \le 3$ ←——+——+——+——+——+——+——+——+——+——→ *x*
   -4 -3 -2 -1 0 1 2 3 4

2. $t > 1$ ←——+——+——+——+——+——+——+——+——+——→ *t*
   -4 -3 -2 -1 0 1 2 3 4

3. $q \ge -10$ ←——+——+——+——+——+——+——+——+——+——→ *q*
   -20   -10   0   10   20

4. $m < 50$ ←——+——+——+——+——+——+——+——+——+——→ *m*
   -10 0 10 20 30 40 50 60 70

For each inequality, tell whether the number in bold is a solution.

5. $x < 7; \mathbf{7}$ _____

6. $p > -3; \mathbf{3}$ _____

7. $k \ge 5; \mathbf{0}$ _____

8. $3z \le 12; \mathbf{4}$ _____

9. $n - 5 > 3; \mathbf{6}$ _____

10. $2g + 8 \ge 3; \mathbf{-1}$ _____

Write an inequality for each graph.

11. _____

   -4 -3 -2 -1 0 1 2 3 4 *x*

12. _____

   -10 0 10 20 30 40 50 60 70 *z*

Write an inequality for each statement. Graph each solution on the number line shown.

13. You can walk there in 20 minutes or less.

_____

←——+——+——+——+——+——+——+——+——+——→ *t*
0 5 10 15 20 25 30 35 40

14. Each prize is worth over $150.

_____

←——+——+——+——+——+——+——+——+——→ *v*
0   100   200   300   400

15. A species of catfish, *malapterurus electricus*, can generate up to 350 volts of electricity.

  a. Write an inequality to represent the amount of electricity generated by the catfish.

  _____

  b. Draw a graph of the inequality you wrote in **a.**

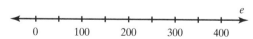
←——+——+——+——+——+——+——→ *e*
0   100   200   300   400

3-1 • Guided Problem Solving

GPS **Student Page 103, Exercise 30:**

Reasoning Explain why $-17 > -22$.

Understand

1. What are you being asked to do?

   _____

   _____

2. What visual representation can you use to help your explanation?

   _____

Plan and Carry Out

3. Graph -17 on a number line.

   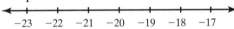

   $-23 \quad -22 \quad -21 \quad -20 \quad -19 \quad -18 \quad -17$

4. Graph -22 on the same number line.

5. Which number is farther to the right on the number line?

   _____

6. Why is $-17 > -22$?

   _____

   _____

Check

7. Which mathematical definition did you use to explain that $-17 > -22$?

   _____

   _____

Solve Another Problem

8. Explain why $-8 < -5$.

   _____

   _____

Practice 3-2

Solving Inequalities by Adding or Subtracting

Solve each inequality. Graph each solution.

1. $w + 4 < -2$

_____

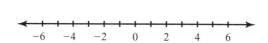

2. $a - 4 \geq 0$

_____

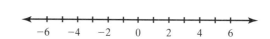

3. $a + 19 > 13$

_____

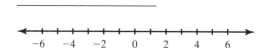

4. $x + 7 \leq 12$

_____

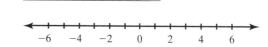

5. $a + 2 > -3$

_____

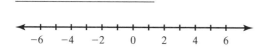

6. $t - 6 < 3$

_____

7. $r - 3.4 \leq 2.6$

_____

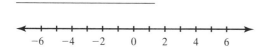

8. $a + 5.7 \geq -2.3$

_____

9. $h - 4.9 > -0.9$

_____

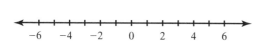

10. $y + 3.4 < -4.6$

_____

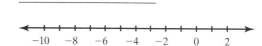

Write an inequality for each problem. Solve the inequality.

11. The school record for the most points scored in a football season is 85. Lawrence has 44 points so far this season. How many more points does he need to break the record?

_____

_____

12. The maximum weight limit for a fully loaded truck is 16,000 pounds. The truck you are loading currently weighs 12,500 pounds. How much more weight can be added and not exceed the weight limit?

_____

_____

3-2 • Guided Problem Solving ....

GPS **Student Page 106, Exercise 27:**

Consumer Issues Your parents give you $35 for a scooter that costs at least $100. How much money do you have to save to buy the scooter?

Understand

1. Circle the information you will need to solve this problem.

2. What are you being asked to do?

   _____

   _____

3. What expression would you use to represent the phrase "*at least* $100?"

   _____

Plan and Carry Out

Suppose the scooter costs *at least* $100.

4. Write an expression for the amount of money you need to save, *s*, plus the amount of money your parents will give you.

   _____

5. How much money do you need to buy the scooter?

   _____

6. Write an inequality to solve for *s*. _____

7. Solve the inequality. _____

8. How much money do you have to save for the scooter?

   _____

Check

9. If you save $65, how much money will you have?

   _____

Solve Another Problem

10. You have to be at least 42 in. tall to ride the big roller coasters at the amusement park. You are 36 in. tall right now. How much more do you have to grow? Write and solve an inequality.

    _____

Practice 3-3

Solving Inequalities by Multiplying or Dividing

Solve each inequality. Graph each solution.

1. $6w \le 36$

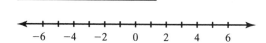

2. $10a \ge 40$

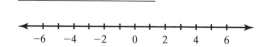

3. $\dfrac{f}{3} \le -2$

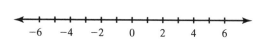

4. $\dfrac{v}{4} > 2$

5. $7a > -28$

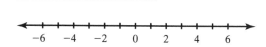

6. $-\dfrac{c}{3} \ge 3$

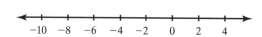

7. $\dfrac{f}{2} > -1$

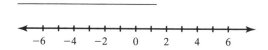

8. $9a \le 63$

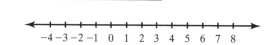

9. $4w \ge -12$

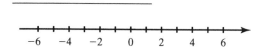

10. $-\dfrac{h}{2} \ge -5$

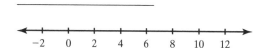

Write an inequality to solve each problem. Then solve the inequality.

11. Marcus wants to buy 5 baseballs. He has $35. What is the most each baseball can cost?

_____

_____

_____

12. Melinda charges $4 per hour for babysitting. Mrs. Garden does not want to spend more than $25 for babysitting. What is the maximum number of hours that she can have Melinda babysit?

_____

_____

_____

3-3 • Guided Problem Solving

GPS **Student Page 112, Exercise 23:**

Rides A roller coaster can carry 36 people per run. How many times does the roller coaster have to run to allow at least 10,000 people to ride?

Understand

1. Circle the information you will need to solve this problem.

2. What are you being asked to do?

   _____

   _____

3. What symbol would you use to represent the phrase *at least 10,000 people*?

   _____

Plan and Carry Out

4. Write an expression for the maximum number of people who could ride the roller coaster in *r* runs.

   _____

5. At least how many people need to ride? _____

6. Write an inequality to solve for *r*. _____

7. Solve the inequality. _____

8. How many times does the roller coaster
   need to run?   _____

Check

9. If the roller coaster runs 278 times, how many people will it have carried? Use a calculator to check your answer.

   _____

Solve Another Problem

10. Chicken is on sale for $1.99 per pound. The most you can spend is $20, and you must buy a whole number of pounds. How many pounds of chicken can you buy?

    _____

Name _____ Class _____ Date _____

Practice 3-4 Solving Two-Step Inequalities

Solve each inequality. Graph the solution. Write your answer in simplest form.

1. $-3 + 5n > -13$

2. $4 \geq \frac{z}{3} - 1$

3. $6 - 4b \leq 14$

4. $5t + 2 < 7$

5. $\frac{s}{4} + 3 \geq 9$

6. $-7b + 2 < 16$

Solve each inequality. Circle the letter of the inequality that is represented by each graph.

7.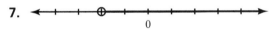

A. $4d - 3 < 9$ **B.** $-2d + 4 < 8$

8.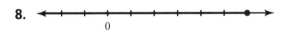

A. $6 - 1.5x \geq -3$ **B.** $-2.4x + 3.2 \geq -4$

9. Tasha gets \$7.50 every week for walking the neighbor's dog daily. She also makes and sells bracelets for \$2.50 each. She wants to earn at least \$25 this week as vacation money. Write an inequality to find the number of bracelets she needs to make. Graph and describe the solutions.

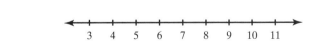

3-4 • Guided Problem Solving

Student Page 119, Exercise 27:

Event Planning A play is being presented in a school gymnasium that can hold a maximum of 600 people. One hundred twenty people can sit on the bleachers. Chairs will be set up in 15 equal rows. Describe the number of chairs that can be in each row.

Understand

1. Circle the information you will need to solve the problem.

2. What are you being asked to do? _____
_____

Plan and Carry Out

3. What is the maximum number of people you must plan for? _____
_____

4. Write an expression to show the number of chairs in each row, *c*.
_____

5. How many people can sit on the bleachers? _____
_____

6. What inequality can you use to solve for *c*? _____

7. How many chairs will be placed in each row? _____
_____

Check

8. Explain why your answer is correct. _____
_____
_____
_____

Solve Another Problem

9. Scott plans to fill an empty room in his greenhouse. The room can hold a maximum of 80 plants. Twenty plants can be hung from the ceiling racks. The rest of the plants can be placed in 4 equal rows on the table. Describe the number of plants that can be in each row.

_____

_____

Name _____ Class _____ Date _____

3A: Graphic Organizer

For use before Lesson 3-1

Study Skill You should fully understand the basic concepts in each chapter before moving on to more complex material. Be sure to ask questions when you are not comfortable with what you have learned.

Write your answers.

1. What is the chapter title? _____

2. How many lessons are there in this chapter? _____

3. What is the topic of the Test-Taking Strategies page? _____

4. Complete the graphic organizer below as you work through the chapter.
   - In the center, write the title of the chapter.
   - When you begin a lesson, write the lesson name in a rectangle.
   - When you complete a lesson, write a skill or key concept in a circle linked to that lesson block.
   - When you complete the chapter, use this graphic organizer to help you review.

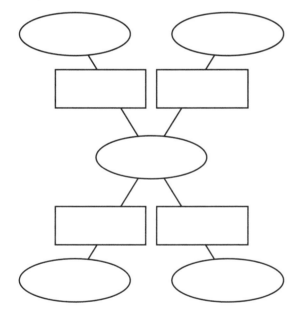

3B: Reading Comprehension

Study Skill As you learn more vocabulary, more concepts are within your reach.

Read the paragraph below and answer the questions that follow.

November is American Indian and Alaska Native Heritage Month. According to the U.S. Census Bureau, more than 4 million people in the United States identified themselves as American Indian or Alaska native in 2004. That is 1.5% of the total U.S. population. About 687,000 people with this heritage live in California, giving it the largest American Indian and Alaska native population of any state. However, $\frac{1}{5}$ of the Alaska population is American Indian or Alaska native. This is a much greater fraction than in California.

1. What is the subject of this paragraph?

   _____

   _____

2. What is the largest number in the paragraph?

   _____

3. What is the smallest number?

   _____

4. Which state has the greatest number of people with American Indian and Alaska native ancestry?

   _____

5. The population of Alaska is about 665,000. How many Alaskans have American Indian or Alaska native heritage?

   _____

6. Explain how California can have the greatest population but not the largest fraction of people with this ancestry.

   _____

7. **High-Use Academic Words** In Exercise 6, what does the word *explain* mean?

   a. to put or use in place of something else

   b. to give facts and details that make an idea easier to understand

3C: Reading/Writing Math Symbols

For use after Lesson 3-3

Vocabulary and Study Skills

Study Skill Read problems carefully. Pay special attention to units when working with measurements.

Match the abbreviation in Column A with the name of the unit in Column B.

Column A	Column B
1. 1b	**A.** mile
2. in.	**B.** pound
3. mi	**C.** calorie
4. s	**D.** gram
5. min	**E.** meter
6. cal	**F.** inch
7. g	**G.** minute
8. m	**H.** second

Describe what the symbol on each number line means.

9.
10

_____

10.
10

_____

11.
10

_____

12.
10

_____

3D: Visual Vocabulary Practice

Study Skill Making sense of mathematical symbols is like reading a foreign language that uses different letters.

Concept List

Addition Property of Inequality	Subtraction Property of Inequality
Division Property of Inequality	Multiplication Property of Inequality
reciprocal	quotient
product	solution of an inequality
inequality	

Write the concept that best describes each exercise. Choose from the concept list above.

1. If $6x > 84$, then $\dfrac{6x}{6} > \dfrac{84}{6}$.	2. $8 + x \geq 2x$	3. 15 in the equation $x \div 7 = 15$. 27 in the equation $\dfrac{m}{8} = 27$.
4. For $\dfrac{1}{7}$, it is 7. For $\dfrac{8}{3}$, it is $\dfrac{3}{8}$. For 9, it is $\dfrac{1}{9}$.	5. If $7m < 1 + 2m$, then $7m - 2m < 1 + 2m - 2m$.	6. For 7 and 12, it is 84. For 14 and x, it is $14x$.
7. In $x - 27 > 41$, then $x - 27 + 27 > 41 + 27$.	8. $-2x + 1 < 4$ $-2x < 3$ $x > -\dfrac{3}{2}$ 0 represents this for $-2x + 1 < 4$.	9. If $\dfrac{1}{9}z < 8$, then $9 \times \left(\dfrac{1}{9}z\right) < 9 \times 8$.

3E: Vocabulary Check

Study Skill Strengthen your vocabulary. Use these pages and add cues and summaries by applying the Cornell Notetaking style.

Write the definition for each word or term at the right. To check your work, fold the paper back along the dotted line to see the correct answers.

_____

_____

_____ quotient

_____

_____

_____ inequality

_____

_____

_____ reciprocals

_____

_____

_____ product

_____

_____

_____ compound inequality

_____

_____

Vocabulary and Study Skills

3E: Vocabulary Check (continued)   **For use after Lesson 3-4**

Write the definition for each word or term at the right. To check your work, fold the paper forward along the dotted line to see the correct answers.

the solution to a division sentence

_____

a mathematical sentence that contains $<, >, \leq, \geq,$ or $\neq$

_____

two numbers whose product is 1

_____

the solution to a multiplication sentence

_____

a number sentence with more than one inequality symbol

_____

3F: Vocabulary Review

For use with the Chapter Review

Study Skill Review notes that you have taken in class as soon as possible to clarify any points you missed and to refresh your memory.

Circle the word that best completes the sentence.

1. A mathematical statement that contains $<$ or $>$ is called an (*equation, inequality*).

2. You use the (*Addition, Multiplication*) Property of Inequality if you add the same value to each side of an inequality.

3. Two numbers are (*inverses, reciprocals*) if their product is 1.

4. The solution to a division sentence is a (*quotient, divisor*).

5. If you use the (*Division, Subtraction*) Property of Inequality with a negative number, the direction of the inequality symbol is reversed.

6. You can use the (*Multiplication, Addition*) Property of Inequality to solve the inequality $m \div 6 < 29$.

7. You use the (*Subtraction, Division*) Property of Inequality if you take away the same value from each side of an inequality.

8. To solve an inequality involving addition, you use (*subtraction, reciprocals*).

9. When solving a two-step inequality, you need to get the (*variable, reciprocal*) along on one side of the inequality.

10. A (*variable, solution*) of an inequality is any value that makes the inequality true.

11. A number sentence is a (*compound, rational*) inequality if it has more than one inequality symbol.

12. The solution to a multiplication sentence is a (*product, difference*).

Name _____ Class _____ Date _____

Practice 4-1 Ratios

Write a ratio for each situation in three ways.

1. Ten years ago in Louisiana, schools averaged 182 pupils for every 10 teachers.

_____

2. Between 1899 and 1900, 284 out of 1,000 people in the United States were 5–17 years old.

_____

Use the chart below for Exercises 3–4.

Three seventh-grade classes were asked whether they wanted chicken or pasta served at their awards banquet.

Room Number	Chicken	Pasta
201	10	12
202	8	17
203	16	10

3. In room 201, what is the ratio of students who prefer chicken to students who prefer pasta?

_____

4. Combine the totals for all three rooms. What is the ratio of the number of students who prefer pasta to the number of students who prefer chicken?

_____

Write each ratio as a fraction in simplest form.

5. 12 to 18 _____

6. 81 : 27 _____

7. $\frac{6}{28}$ _____

Tell whether the ratios are *equivalent* or *not equivalent*.

8. 12 : 24, 50 : 100 _____

9. $\frac{22}{1}, \frac{1}{22}$ _____

10. 2 to 3, 24 to 36 _____

11. A bag contains green, yellow, and orange marbles. The ratio of green marbles to yellow marbles is 2 : 5. The ratio of yellow marbles to orange marbles is 3 : 4. What is the ratio of green marbles to orange marbles?

_____

4-1 • Guided Problem Solving

GPS **Student Page 130, Exercise 27:**

Cooking To make pancakes, you need 2 cups of water for every 3 cups of flour. Write an equivalent ratio to find how much water you will need with 9 cups of flour.

Understand

1. Circle the information you will need to solve.

2. What are you being asked to do?

   _____

   _____

3. Why will a ratio help you to solve the problem?

   _____

   _____

   _____

Plan and Carry Out

4. What is the ratio of the cups of water to the cups of flour?   _____

5. How many cups of flour are you using?   _____

6. Write an equivalent ratio to use 9 cups of flour.   _____

7. How many cups of water are needed for 9 cups of flour?   _____

Check

8. Why is the number of cups of water triple the number of cups needed for 3 cups of flour?

   _____

   _____

Solve Another Problem

9. Rebecca is laying tile in her bathroom. She needs 4 black tiles for every 16 white tiles. How many black tiles are needed if she uses 128 white tiles?

   _____

Practice 4-2

Unit Rates and Proportional Reasoning

Write the unit rate for each situation.

1. travel 250 mi in 5 h

_____

2. earn $75.20 in 8 h

_____

3. read 80 pages in 2 h

_____

4. type 8,580 words in 2 h 45 min

_____

5. complete $\frac{3}{4}$ of a puzzle in $\frac{7}{8}$ h

_____

6. drink $\frac{4}{5}$ L in $\frac{1}{4}$ h

_____

Find each unit price. Then determine the better buy.

7. paper: 100 sheets for $.99
       500 sheets for $4.29

_____

8. peanuts: 1 lb for $1.29
       12 oz for $.95

_____

9. crackers: 15 oz for $1.79
       12 oz for $1.49

_____

10. apples: 3 lb for $1.89
        5 lb for $2.49

_____

11. mechanical pencils: 4 for $1.25
        25 for $5.69

_____

12. bagels: 4 for $.89
        6 for $1.39

_____

13. a. Yolanda and Yoko ran in a 100-yd dash. When Yolanda crossed the finish line, Yoko was 10 yd behind her. The girls then repeated the race, with Yolanda starting 10 yd behind the starting line. If each girl ran at the same rate as before, who won the race? By how many yards?

_____

b. Assuming the girls run at the same rate as before, how far behind the starting line should Yolanda be in order for the two to finish in a tie?

_____

Name _____ Class _____ Date _____

4-2 • Guided Problem Solving

Geography Population density is the number of people per unit of area. Alaska has the lowest population density of any state in the United States. It has 626,932 people in 570,374 mi^2. What is its population density? Round to the nearest person per square mile.

Understand

1. What is *population density*?

_____

_____

2. What are you being asked to do?

_____

3. What does the phrase *people per unit of area* imply?

_____

_____

_____

Plan and Carry Out

4. What is the population of Alaska?   _____

5. What is the area of Alaska?   _____

6. Write a division expression for the population density.   _____

7. What is its population density?   _____

8. Round to the nearest person per square mile.   _____

Check

9. Why is the population density only about 1 person/mi^2?

_____

_____

Solve Another Problem

10. Mr. Boyle is buying pizza for the percussion band. The bill is $56.82 for 5 pizzas. If there are 12 members of the band, how much does the pizza cost per member? Round to the nearest cent.

_____

_____

Name _____ Class _____ Date _____

Practice 4-3

Proportions

Determine if the ratios in each pair are proportional.

1. $\frac{12}{16}, \frac{30}{40}$ _____

2. $\frac{8}{12}, \frac{15}{21}$ _____

3. $\frac{27}{21}, \frac{81}{56}$ _____

4. $\frac{45}{24}, \frac{75}{40}$ _____

5. $\frac{5}{9}, \frac{80}{117}$ _____

6. $\frac{15}{25}, \frac{75}{125}$ _____

7. $\frac{2}{14}, \frac{20}{35}$ _____

8. $\frac{9}{6}, \frac{21}{14}$ _____

9. $\frac{24}{15}, \frac{16}{10}$ _____

10. $\frac{3}{4}, \frac{8}{10}$ _____

11. $\frac{20}{4}, \frac{17}{3}$ _____

12. $\frac{25}{6}, \frac{9}{8}$ _____

Decide if each pair of ratios is proportional.

13. $\frac{14}{10} \stackrel{?}{=} \frac{9}{7}$

_____

14. $\frac{18}{8} \stackrel{?}{=} \frac{36}{16}$

_____

15. $\frac{6}{10} \stackrel{?}{=} \frac{15}{25}$

_____

16. $\frac{7}{16} \stackrel{?}{=} \frac{4}{9}$

_____

17. $\frac{6}{4} \stackrel{?}{=} \frac{12}{8}$

_____

18. $\frac{19}{3} \stackrel{?}{=} \frac{114}{8}$

_____

19. $\frac{5}{14} \stackrel{?}{=} \frac{6}{15}$

_____

20. $\frac{6}{27} \stackrel{?}{=} \frac{8}{36}$

_____

21. $\frac{27}{15} \stackrel{?}{=} \frac{45}{25}$

_____

22. $\frac{3}{18} \stackrel{?}{=} \frac{4}{20}$

_____

23. $\frac{5}{2} \stackrel{?}{=} \frac{15}{6}$

_____

24. $\frac{20}{15} \stackrel{?}{=} \frac{4}{3}$

_____

Solve.

25. During the breaststroke competitions of the 1992 Olympics, Nelson Diebel swam 100 meters in 62 seconds, and Mike Bowerman swam 200 meters in 130 seconds. Are the rates proportional?

_____

26. During a vacation, the Vasquez family traveled 174 miles in 3 hours on Monday, and 290 miles in 5 hours on Tuesday. Are the rates proportional?

_____

4-3 • Guided Problem Solving

GPS **Student Page 139, Exercise 29:**

Decorating A certain shade of green paint requires 4 parts blue to 5 parts yellow. If you mix 16 quarts of blue paint with 25 quarts of yellow paint, will you get the desired shade of green? Explain.

Understand

1. Circle the information you will need to solve.

2. What are you being asked to do?

_____

_____

3. Will a ratio help you to solve the problem? Explain.

_____

_____

Plan and Carry Out

4. What is the ratio of blue parts to yellow parts? _____

5. What is the ratio of blue quarts to yellow quarts? _____

6. Check to see if the cross products of the two ratios are equal.

_____

7. Are the ratios the same? _____

8. Will you get the desired shade of green? Explain.

_____

Check

9. How do you know that the ratios are not the same?

_____

Solve Another Problem

10. There are 15 boys and 12 girls in your math class. There are 5 boys and 3 girls in your study group. Determine if the boy to girl ratio is the same in study group as it is in your math class. Explain.

_____

_____

Practice 4-4

Solving Proportions

Use mental math to solve for each value of *n*.

1. $\dfrac{n}{14} = \dfrac{20}{35}$ _____

2. $\dfrac{9}{6} = \dfrac{21}{n}$ _____

3. $\dfrac{24}{n} = \dfrac{16}{10}$ _____

4. $\dfrac{3}{4} = \dfrac{n}{10}$ _____

Solve each proportion using cross products.

5. $\dfrac{k}{8} = \dfrac{14}{4}$

$k =$ _____

6. $\dfrac{u}{3} = \dfrac{10}{5}$

$u =$ _____

7. $\dfrac{14}{6} = \dfrac{d}{15}$

$d =$ _____

8. $\dfrac{5}{1} = \dfrac{m}{4}$

$m =$ _____

9. $\dfrac{36}{32} = \dfrac{n}{8}$

$n =$ _____

10. $\dfrac{5}{30} = \dfrac{1}{x}$

$x =$ _____

11. $\dfrac{t}{4} = \dfrac{5}{10}$

$t =$ _____

12. $\dfrac{9}{2} = \dfrac{v}{4}$

$v =$ _____

Solve.

13. A contractor estimates it will cost $2,400 to build a deck to a customer's specifications. How much would it cost to build five similar decks?

_____

14. A recipe requires 3 c of flour to make 27 dinner rolls. How much flour is needed to make 9 rolls?

_____

Solve using a calculator, paper and pencil, or mental math.

15. Mandy runs 4 km in 18 min. She plans to run in a 15 km race. How long will it take her to complete the race?

_____

16. Ken's new car can go 26 miles per gallon of gasoline. The car's gasoline tank holds 14 gal. How far will he be able to go on a full tank?

_____

17. Eleanor can complete two skirts in 15 days. How long will it take her to complete eight skirts?

_____

18. Three eggs are required to make two dozen muffins. How many eggs are needed to make 12 dozen muffins?

_____

4-4 • Guided Problem Solving

GPS Student Page 146, Exercise 28:

There are 450 students and 15 teachers in a school. The school hires 2 new teachers. To keep the student-to-teacher ratio the same, how many students in all should attend the school?

Understand

1. What are you being asked to do?

_____

_____

2. Will a proportion help you to solve the problem? Explain.

_____

_____

_____

Plan and Carry Out

3. Write a ratio for the current student-to-teacher ratio. _____

4. Write a ratio for the new student-to-teacher ratio. _____

5. Write a proportion using the ratios in Steps 3 and 4. _____

6. How many total students should attend the school?

_____

Check

7. Are the two ratios equivalent? Explain.

_____

_____

Solve Another Problem

8. There are 6 black marbles and 4 red marbles in a jar. If you add 4 red marbles to the jar, how many black marbles do you need to add to keep the ratio of black marbles to red marbles the same?

_____

Guided Problem Solving

Name _____ Class _____ Date _____

Practice 4-5

Similar Figures

$\triangle MNO \sim \triangle JKL$. **Complete each statement.**

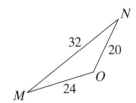

1. $\angle M$ corresponds to _____.   **2.** $\angle L$ corresponds to _____.

3. $\overline{JL}$ corresponds to _____.   **4.** $\overline{MN}$ corresponds to _____.

5. What is the ratio of the lengths of the corresponding sides? _____

The pairs of figures below are similar. Find the value of each variable.

6.
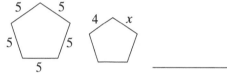
_____

7.
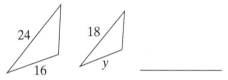
_____

8.
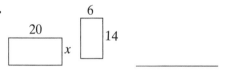
_____

9.
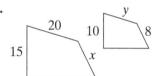
_____

10.
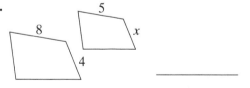
_____

11.
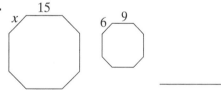
_____

12. On a sunny day, if a 36-inch yardstick casts a 21-inch shadow, how tall is a building whose shadow is 168 ft?

_____

13. Oregon is about 400 miles from west to east, and 300 miles from north to south. If a map of Oregon is 15 inches tall (from north to south), about how wide is the map?

_____

4-5 • Guided Problem Solving

GPS Student Page 153, Exercise 13:

Geometry A rectangle with an area of 32 in^2 has one side measuring 4 in. A similar rectangle has an area of 288 in^2. How long is the longer side in the larger rectangle?

Understand

1. What are you being asked to do?

   _____

2. Will a proportion that equates the ratio of the areas to the ratio of the shorter sides result in the desired answer? Explain.

   _____

   _____

   _____

3. What measure should you determine first?

   _____

   _____

Plan and Carry Out

4. What is the length of the longer side of the rectangle whose area is 32 in.^{2} and whose shorter side is 4 in.? _____

5. What is the ratio of the longer side to the shorter side? _____

6. What pairs of factors multiply to equal 288?

   _____

7. Which pair of factors has a ratio of $\frac{2}{1}$? _____

8. What is the length of the longer side? _____

Check

9. Why must the ratio between the factors be $\frac{2}{1}$?

   _____

   _____

Solve Another Problem

10. A triangle with perimeter 26 in. has two sides that are 8 in. long. What is the length of the third side of a similar triangle which has two sides that are 12 in. long? _____

Guided Problem Solving

Name _____ Class _____ Date _____

Practice 4-6   Maps and Scale Drawings

The scale of a map is 2 cm : 21 km. Find the actual distances for the following map distances.

1. 9 cm _____   **2.** 12.5 cm _____   **3.** 14 mm _____

4. 3.6 m _____   **5.** 4.5 cm _____   **6.** 7.1 cm _____

A scale drawing has a scale of $\frac{1}{4}$ in. : 12 ft. Find the length on the drawing for each actual length.

7. 8 ft _____   **8.** 30 ft _____   **9.** 15 ft _____

10. 18 ft _____   **11.** 20 ft _____   **12.** 40 ft _____

Use a metric ruler to find the approximate distance between the towns.

13. Hickokburg to Kidville _____

14. Dodgetown to Earp City _____

15. Dodgetown to Kidville _____

16. Kidville to Earp City _____

17. Dodgetown to Hickokburg _____

18. Earp City to Hickokburg _____

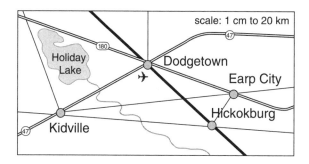

Solve.

19. The scale drawing shows a two-bedroom apartment. The master bedroom is 9 ft × 12 ft. Use an inch ruler to measure the drawing.

    a. The scale is _____ .

    b. Write the actual dimensions in place of the scale dimensions.

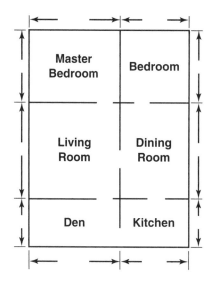

4-6 • Guided Problem Solving

GPS **Student Page 161, Exercise 23:**

Writing in Math You are making a scale drawing with a scale of
2 in. = 17 ft. Explain how you find the length of the drawing of an
object that has an actual length of 51 ft.

Understand

1. What are you being asked to do?

   _____

   _____

2. What points should you include in your explanation?

   _____

   _____

3. What is a scale?

   _____

   _____

Plan and Carry Out

4. What is the scale? _____

5. What is the actual length of the object? _____

6. Write a proportion using the scale, the actual
   length, and the unknown length of the drawing. _____

7. What is the length of the object in a drawing? _____

Check

8. Use Steps 4–7 to explain how you decided how long to draw the
   object.

   _____

   _____

   _____

Solve Another Problem

9. The length of the wing of a model airplane is 3 in.
   If the scale of the model to the actual plane is
   1 in. = 25 ft, what is the length of the actual wing? _____

Name _____ Class _____ Date _____

Practice 4-7

Proportional Relationships

Determine whether each table or graph represents a proportional relationship. Explain your reasoning.

1.

x	1	3	6	8	9
y	4.5	13.5	24	36	38

_____

_____

2.

x	1	5	8	11	12
y	$\frac{8}{5}$	$\frac{40}{5}$	$\frac{64}{5}$	$\frac{88}{5}$	$\frac{96}{5}$

_____

_____

3.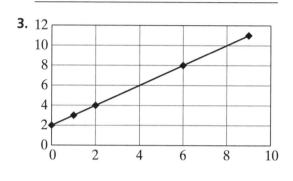

_____

_____

4.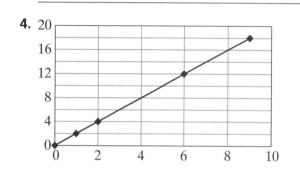

_____

_____

Find the constant of proportionality for each table of values.

5.

Roses	6	12	24
Price	$22.50	$45.00	$90.00

$c =$ _____

6.

Tomatoes (lb)	3	7	9
Price	$4.47	$10.43	$13.41

$c =$ _____

7.

Gallons	5	10	15
Miles	120	240	360

$c =$ _____

8.

Seconds	2	6	8
Feet	500	1,500	2,000

$c =$ _____

Write an equation using the constant of proportionality to describe the relationship.

9. A boat that has traveled 8 leagues from shore is 24 nautical miles out. Find the number of miles m in l leagues. _____

10. Four score years ago is 80 years past. Find the number of years y in s scores. _____

4-7 • Guided Problem Solving

GPS Student Page 168, Exercise 15:

Error Analysis A salesperson showed the table below while explaining that oranges are the same price per pound, no matter what size bag they come in. Why is the salesperson wrong?

$	$8	$10	$20
lbs	4	6	10

Understand

1. What are you being asked to do?

   _____

   _____

2. What will you use to find the answer?

   _____

   _____

Plan and Carry Out

3. What is the unit price for 4 pounds of oranges? _____

4. What is the unit price for 6 pounds of oranges? _____

5. What is the unit price for 10 pounds of oranges? _____

6. Why is the salesperson wrong?

   _____

   _____

Check

7. How can you check your answer?

   _____

   _____

Solve Another Problem

8. A customer thinks pizzas cost the same per slice at a local restaurant. Why is the customer wrong?

   _____

   _____

$	$8	$9	$12
Slices	10	12	16

4A: Graphic Organizer

For use before Lesson 4-1

Study Skill As you read over the material in the chapter, keep a paper and pencil handy to write down notes and questions in your math notebook. Review notes taken in class as soon as possible.

Write your answers.

1. What is the chapter title? _____

2. How many lessons are there in this chapter? _____

3. What is the topic of the Test-Taking Strategies page? _____

4. Complete the graphic organizer below as you work through the chapter.

   • In the center, write the title of the chapter.

   • When you begin a lesson, write the lesson name in a rectangle.

   • When you complete a lesson, write a skill or key concept in a circle linked to that lesson block.

   • When you complete the chapter, use this graphic organizer to help you review.

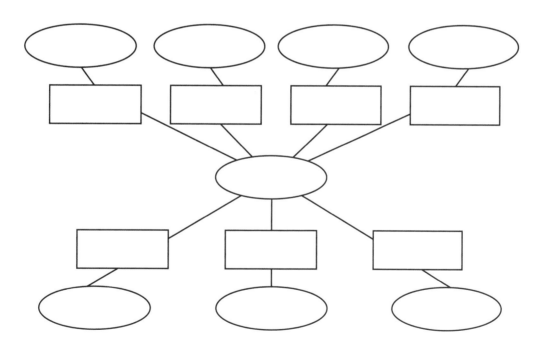

4B: Reading Comprehension

For use after Lesson 4-3

Study Skill When you read mathematics, look for words like "more than," "less than," "above," "times as many," "divided by." These clues will help you decide what operation you need to solve a problem.

Read the paragraph and answer the questions that follow.

> A tropical storm is classified as a hurricane when it has wind speeds in excess of 74 mi/h. The winds of Hurricane Gordon (1994) reached 12.4 mi/h above the minimum. How fast were the winds of Hurricane Gordon?

1. What numbers are in the paragraph? _____

2. What question are you asked to answer? _____
   _____

3. What units will you use in your answer? _____

4. Does a storm with winds of 74 mi/h qualify as a hurricane? Explain.
   _____
   _____
   _____

5. When did Hurricane Gordon occur? _____

6. How much above the minimum were Hurricane Gordon's winds?
   _____

7. Let *x* represent Hurricane Gordon's wind speed. Write an equation to help you solve the problem.
   _____

8. What is the answer to the question asked in the paragraph?
   _____

9. **High-Use Academic Words** In Exercise 7, what does it mean to *solve*?
   a. to find an answer for   **b.** to keep something going

4C: Reading/Writing Math Symbols · · · · · · · · · · · · · · For use after Lesson 4-4

Study Skill When you take notes in any subject, use abbreviations and symbols whenever possible.

Write each statement or expression using the appropriate mathematical symbols.

1. the ratio of a to b _____

2. x to 4 is less than 5 to 2 _____

3. 4 more than 5 times n _____

4. $5:24$ is not equal to $1:5$ _____

Write each mathematical statement in words.

5. $x \le 25$

_____

_____

6. $|-20| > |15|$

_____

_____

_____

7. $1 \text{ oz} \approx 28 \text{ g}$

_____

_____

8. $\frac{1}{3} = \frac{4}{12}$

_____

_____

Match the symbolic statement or expression in Column A with its written form in Column B.

Column A	Column B
9. $k < 12$	**A.** 12 times x
10. $|-5|$	**B.** negative 2 plus negative 4 is p
11. $n \ge 15$	**C.** the ratio of 4 to 8
12. $x = -4 + 5$	**D.** k is less than 12
13. $4:8$	**E.** the quotient of x and 9
14. $12x$	**F.** x equals negative 4 plus 5
15. $-2 + (-4) = p$	**G.** the absolute value of negative 5
16. $x \div 9$	**H.** n is greater than or equal to 15

4D: Visual Vocabulary Practice

Study Skill When you come across something you don't understand, view it as an opportunity to increase your brain power.

Concept List

cross products	equivalent ratios	indirect measurement
proportion	rate	scale
similar polygons	unit cost	unit rate

Write the concept that best describes each exercise. Choose from the concept list above.

1. $\frac{18}{16}$ and 4.5 : 4	2. A 6-ft-tall person standing near a building has a shadow that is 60 ft long. This can be used to determine the height of the building.	3. A bakery sells a dozen donuts for $3.15. This can also be represented as $\frac{\$3.15}{12 \text{ donuts}}$.
4. The expression "45 words per minute" represents this.	5. $\frac{30}{75} = \frac{2}{5}$	6. For the equation $\frac{15}{16} = \frac{3z}{4}$, these are represented by 15×4 and $3z \times 16$.
7. The equation $\frac{1}{2}$ in. = 50 mi represents this on a map.	8. $\frac{\$4.25}{5 \text{ lb}} = \frac{\$0.85}{\text{lb}}$	9.

4E: Vocabulary Check

For use after Lesson 4-7

Study Skill Strengthen your vocabulary. Use these pages and add cues and summaries by applying the Cornell Notetaking style.

Write the definition for each word or term at the right. To check your work, fold the paper back along the dotted line to see the correct answers.

_____ polygon

_____
_____

_____ proportion
_____
_____

_____ unit rate
_____
_____

_____ ratio
_____
_____

_____ scale drawing
_____
_____

Vocabulary and Study Skills

4E: Vocabulary Check (continued) · · · · · · · · · · · · For use after Lesson 4-7

Write the vocabulary word or term for each definition. To check your work, fold the paper forward along the dotted line to see the correct answers.

a closed figure formed by three or more line segments that do not cross

_____

an equation stating that two ratios are equal

_____

the rate for one unit of a given quantity

_____

a comparison of two quantities by division

_____

an enlarged or reduced drawing of an object that is similar to the actual object

_____

4F: Vocabulary Review Puzzle

For use with the Chapter Review

Study Skill Use a special notebook or section of a loose-leaf binder for math.

Complete the crossword puzzle. For help, use the Glossary in your textbook.

Here are the words you will use to complete this crossword puzzle:

equation	factor	figures	fraction
inequality	mixed number	prime	proportion
ratio	scale drawing		

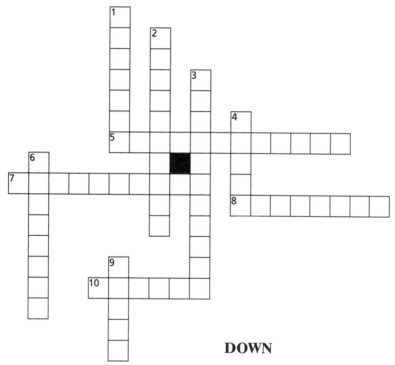

Vocabulary and Study Skills

ACROSS

5. enlarged or reduced drawing of an object

7. equation stating two ratios are equal

8. a statement of two equal expressions

10. a whole number that divides another whole number evenly

DOWN

1. Similar _____ have the same shape but not necessarily the same size.

2. a statement that two expressions are not equal

3. a number made up of a nonzero whole number and a fraction

4. a number with only two factors, one and itself

6. a number in the form $\frac{a}{b}$

9. a comparison of two numbers by division

Name _____ Class _____ Date _____

Practice 5-1

Percents, Fractions, and Decimals

Write each percent as a fraction in simplest form and as a decimal.

1. 65% _____ **2.** 37.5% _____ **3.** 80% _____ **4.** 25% _____

5. 18% _____ **6.** 46% _____ **7.** 87% _____ **8.** 8% _____

9. 43% _____ **10.** 55% _____ **11.** 94% _____ **12.** 36% _____

Write each number as a percent. Round to the nearest tenth of a percent where necessary.

13. $\frac{8}{15}$ _____ **14.** $\frac{7}{50}$ _____ **15.** 0.56 _____

16. 0.0413 _____ **17.** $\frac{3}{8}$ _____ **18.** $\frac{7}{12}$ _____

19. 0.387 _____ **20.** 0.283 _____ **21.** $\frac{2}{9}$ _____

Write each number as a percent. Place the number into the puzzle without using the percent sign or decimal point.

22.

Across	Down
1. 0.134	2. 0.346
3. $\frac{53}{100}$	4. 0.324
5. 0.565	5. $\frac{1}{2}$
7. $1\frac{7}{50}$	6. 0.515
9. 0.456	8. $\frac{33}{200}$
10. 0.63	9. 0.4385
11. $\frac{11}{200}$	10. $\frac{659}{1,000}$
13. 0.58	12. $\frac{1,087}{20,000}$
14. $\frac{191}{200}$	15. $\frac{14}{25}$
16. 0.605	

5-1 • Guided Problem Solving

GPS **Student Page 180, Exercise 35:**

Your teacher uses different methods of grading quizzes. Your quiz grades are 85%, $\frac{9}{10}$, $\frac{16}{20}$, 92%, $\frac{21}{25}$, and 79%.

a. Write your quiz grades in order from least to greatest.

b. Find the average percent grade of your quizzes.

Understand

1. What are you being asked to do in part (a)?

   _____

   _____

2. In order to compare the grades, what should you do first?

   _____

   _____

3. Besides knowing the grades of the quizzes, explain what else is needed to find the average.

   _____

Plan and Carry Out

4. What are all your grades in percent form?

   _____

5. Order the grades from smallest to largest.

   _____

6. What is the total of all your grades? _____

7. Find the average percent grade of your six quizzes. _____

Check

8. Does the average grade fall between the smallest and largest grade?

   _____

Solve Another Problem

9. Your classmate had quiz grades of 75%, $\frac{13}{20}$, $\frac{15}{25}$, 89%, $\frac{8}{10}$, and 81%. Order the grades from least to greatest and find the average.

   _____

Name _____ Class _____ Date _____

Practice 5-2

Solving Percent Problems Using Proportions

Use a proportion to solve.

1. 48 is 60% of what number?

2. What is 175% of 85?

_____

_____

3. What percent of 90 is 50?

4. 76 is 80% of what number?

_____

_____

5. What is 50% of 42.88?

6. 96 is 160% of what number?

_____

_____

7. What percent of 24 is 72?

8. What is 85% of 120?

_____

_____

9. What is 80% of 12?

10. 56 is 75% of what number?

_____

_____

Solve.

11. The sale price of a bicycle is $120. This is 75% of the original price. Find the original price.

_____

12. The attendance at a family reunion was 160 people. This was 125% of last year's attendance. How many people attended the reunion last year?

_____

13. A company has 875 employees. On "Half-Price Wednesday," 64% of the employees eat lunch at the company cafeteria. How many employees eat lunch at the cafeteria on Wednesdays?

_____

14. There are 1,295 students attending a small university. There are 714 women enrolled. What percentage of students are women?

_____

Course 2 Lesson 5-2 **185**

5-2 • Guided Problem Solving

GPS **Student Page 184, Exercise 34:**

At the library, you find 9 books on a certain topic. The librarian tells you that 55% of the books on this topic have been signed out. How many books does the library have available on the topic?

Understand

1. Circle the information you will need to solve.

2. What are you being asked to do?

   _____

   _____

3. If 55% of the books on this topic have been signed out, what percent of the books on this topic have *not* been signed out?

   _____

Plan and Carry Out

4. Choose a variable to represent the total number of books the library has on the topic. _____

5. How many books did you find on the topic? _____

6. Write a proportion comparing the percent of books on this topic to the number of books in the library. _____

7. Solve the proportion. _____

8. How many books does the library have on the topic? _____

Check

9. Is 55% of your answer plus 9 equal to your answer?

   _____

Solve Another Problem

10. There are 12,000 people attending a concert. You learn that 20% of the people who bought tickets to the concert did not attend. How many people bought tickets to the concert?

    _____

    _____

Practice 5-3

Solving Percent Problems Using Equations

Write and solve an equation. Round answers to the nearest tenth.

1. What percent of 64 is 48?

2. 16% of 130 is what number?

3. 25% of what number is 24?

4. What percent of 18 is 12?

5. 48% of 83 is what number?

6. 40% of what number is 136?

7. What percent of 530 is 107?

8. 74% of 643 is what number?

9. 62% of what number is 84?

10. What percent of 84 is 50?

11. 37% of 245 is what number?

12. 12% of what number is 105?

Solve.

13. A cafe offers senior citizens a 15% discount off its regular price of $8.95 for the dinner buffet.
  a. What percent of the regular price is the price for senior citizens? _____
  b. What is the price for senior citizens? _____

14. According to a recent government study, the average 15-year-old male gets 11.4% of his daily caloric intake from sugar drinks. If that 15-year-old consumes 2,400 calories each day, how many calories come from sugar drinks? _____

5-3 • Guided Problem Solving

GPS Student Page 188, Exercise 28:

Food You make 72 cookies for a bake sale. This is 20% of the cookies at the bake sale. How many cookies are at the bake sale?

Understand

1. Circle the information you will need to solve.

2. What are you being asked to do?

   _____

3. What word indicates an equal sign?

   _____

Plan and Carry Out

4. Choose a variable to represent the number of cookies at the bake sale. _____

5. What number is 20% of the cookies at the bake sale? _____

6. Write an expression for the phrase, *20% of the cookies at the bake sale.* _____

7. Write an equation using what you wrote in Steps 5 and 6 to find the number of cookies at the bake sale.

   _____

8. Solve the equation. _____

9. How many cookies are at the bake sale? _____

Check

10. Find 20% of your answer. Does it equal 72?

    _____

Solve Another Problem

11. You collect trading cards and so far you have 12 different cards. If this is 30% of the possible cards, how many cards are there to collect?

    _____

Name _____ Class _____ Date _____

Practice 5-4

Find the total cost.

1. $17.50 with a 7% sales tax

2. $21.95 with a 4.25% sales tax

_____

_____

3. The price of a pair of shoes is $85.99 before sales tax. The sales tax is 7.5%. Find the total cost of the shoes. _____

Estimate a 15% tip for each amount.

4. $12.68

5. $18.25

6. $15.00

_____

_____

_____

Find each commission.

7. 2% on $1,500 in sales

8. 8% on $80,000 in sales

9. 5% on $600 in sales

_____

_____

_____

Find the percent error.

A student in a science lab is measuring the density of various materials. Compare the student's finding to the actual density.

Substance	Density g/cm³	Measured Density g/cm³	Percent Error
concrete	2.4	2.46	**10.**
corn kernel	0.4	0.38	**11.**
copper	8.9	9.1	**12.**

Find the registration fee.

10. To cover office expenses, a gymnastics camp charges a registration fee that is 3.4% of the tuition. If tuition is $485, what is the fee? Round to the nearest cent. _____

11. During peak summer season, a whitewater rafting company charges a 15% registration fee to reserve a 6-person raft that rents for $90. How much is the fee? _____

Solve.

12. To recover a large chair in your home, you purchase $9\frac{1}{2}$ yards of upholstery fabric at $11.00 per yard. If there is a 7% sales tax, what is the total cost of the fabric?

_____

5-4 • Guided Problem Solving

GPS **Student Page 196, Exercise 26:**

Sales A store pays a 6% commission on the first $500 in sales and 8% on sales over $500. Find the commission on an $800 sale.

Understand

1. Circle the information you will need to solve.

2. Define commission.

   _____

   _____

3. Which operations do you need to use to solve this problem?

   _____

Plan and Carry Out

4. $800 = $500 + $\underset{\underline{}}{?}$ _____

5. What is 6% of $500?   _____

6. What is 8% of $300?   _____

7. What is the commission on a $800 sale? _____

Check

8. Find 10% of $500 and 10% of $300. Since 6% is a little more than half of 10%, what is half of 10% of 500? Add this with 10% of 30, since 8% is close to 10%. Does your answer make sense?

   _____

Solve Another Problem

9. Dan's uncle asks him to come work for him at his men's clothing store. He will pay him 5% on his first $1,000 in sales and 8% on sales above $1,000. How much will Dan earn if he sells $2,500 in merchandise?

   _____

   _____

Practice 5-5

Simple Interest

Graph the total *simple* interest earned for each account over 5 years.

1. $1,300 at 6.9%   **2.** $11,500 at 12.50%   **3.** $450 at 3%

Find the simple interest earned in each account.

4. $2,000 at 4% for 6 months

5. $10,000 at 10% for 2 years

_____   _____

6. $500 at 3% for 3 months

7. $25,000 at 4.25% for 5 years

_____   _____

Compare the loans.

8. Compare two loans for $5,000. The 5-year loan has a 5% simple interest rate. The 6-year loan has a 4% simple interest rate. Which loan costs less? _____

9. You want to borrow $2,000. You can get 3-year loan with a 15% simple interest rate or a 5-year loan with a 10% simple interest rate. Which loan costs less? _____

10. You want to borrow $720. You can get a 2-year loan with an 8% simple interest rate or a 1-year loan with a 15% simple interest rate. Which loan costs less? _____

Solve.

11. You invest $5,000 in an account earning simple interest. The balance after 6 years is $6,200. What is the interest rate?

_____

12. Suppose you have $300 to invest. One bank offers an annual simple interest rate of 4.5% for a 3-year investment. Another bank offers an annual simple interest rate of 6.8% for a 2-year investment. Which account will earn you more money?

_____

5-5 • Guided Problem Solving

GPS **Student Page 200, Exercise 16:**

You borrow $500 at 18% simple annual interest. You make payments for 6 months. How much do you owe after 6 months?

Understand

1. What is simple interest?

_____

_____

2. What are you being asked to do?

_____

Plan and Carry Out

3. What is the formula for simple interest? _____

4. What is the original principal?   _____

5. What is the interest rate?   _____

6. How much time in years has passed
since the money was borrowed?   _____

7. Substitute the values into the formula.   _____

8. Including principal, how much do you
owe after 6 months?   _____

Check

9. Find the total simple interest on the account after one year. How should this number compare to the interest you calculated above?

_____

_____

_____

Solve Another Problem

10. You borrow $1,050 at 16% annual interest. How much interest have you paid after 5 years?

_____

Practice 5-6

Find each percent of change. State whether the change is an increase or a decrease.

1. A $50 coat is put on sale for $35.

2. Mayelle earns $18,000 a year. After a raise, she earns $19,500.

3. Last year Anthony earned $24,000. After a brief lay-off this year, Anthony's income is $18,500.

4. In 1981, about $1.1 million was lost due to fires. In 1988, the loss was about $9.6 million.

5. In a recent year, certain colleges and universities received about $268 million in aid. Ten years later, they received about $94 million.

6. A coat regularly costing $125 is put on sale for $75.

7. Complete the table.

Enrollment in Center City Schools From 1995 to 2000

Year	Enrollment	Change from Last Year (number of students)	Change from Last Year (%)	Increase or Decrease
1995	18,500	—	—	—
1996	19,300			
1997	19,700			
1998	19,500			
1999	19,870			
2000	19,200			

5-6 • Guided Problem Solving

GPS **Student Page 205, Exercise 29:**

Sports A football player gained 1,200 yd last season and 900 yd this season. Find the percent of change. State whether the change is an increase or a decrease.

Understand

1. What two numbers will you be comparing?

_____

2. Did the football player gain more yards last season or this season?

_____

3. What are you being asked to do?

_____

Plan and Carry Out

4. What is the difference in the number of yards gained last season and this season? _____

5. Write a proportion comparing the difference and the percent of change. _____

6. What are the cross products? _____

7. What number do you divide each side by? _____

8. What is the percent of change? _____

9. Is it a decrease or increase? _____

Check

10. Explain your answer to step 9.

_____

_____

_____

Solve Another Problem

11. In a previous game the school's star basketball player scored 25 points. In today's game he scored 40 points. What was the percent of change in the player's scoring? Is the change an increase or decrease?

_____

5A: Graphic Organizer

For use before Lesson 5-1

Study Skill As you read over the material in the chapter, keep a paper and pencil handy to write down notes and questions that you have.

Write your answers.

1. What is the chapter title? _____

2. How many lessons are there in this chapter? _____

3. What is the topic of the Test-Taking Strategies page? _____

4. Complete the graphic organizer below as you work through the chapter.

   - In the center, write the title of the chapter.

   - When you begin a lesson, write the lesson name in a rectangle.

   - When you complete a lesson, write a skill or key concept in a circle linked to that lesson block.

   - When you complete the chapter, use this graphic organizer to help you review.

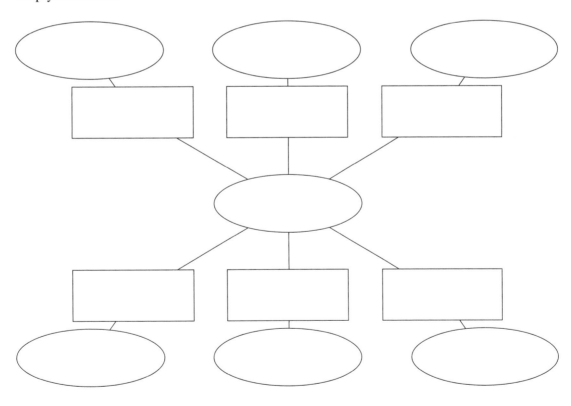

5B: Reading Comprehension

For use after Lesson 5-2

Study Skill Use a special notebook (or section of a loose-leaf binder) for your math handouts and homework. Keep your notebook neat and organized by reviewing its contents often.

Use the graphs shown below to answer the questions that follow.

Reasons given for purchasing rental-car insurance

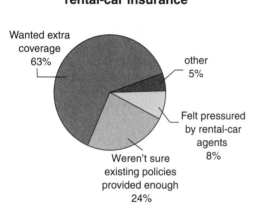

Who buys rental-car insurance

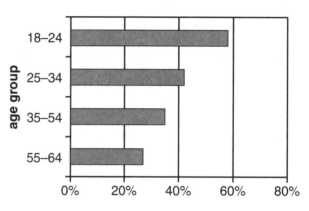

1. What information do the graphs show?

   _____

   _____

2. What is the top reason people purchase rental-car insurance?

   _____

3. What is the total of the percents for reasons people purchase rental-car insurance?

   _____

4. Which age group is most likely to purchase rental-car insurance? _____

5. Approximately $\frac{1}{3}$ of the renters in which age group purchase rental-car insurance?

   _____

6. Approximately $\frac{1}{4}$ of the renters purchase rental-car insurance for what reason?

   _____

7. **High-Use Academic Words** In Exercise 1, what does the word *show* mean?

   a. to display   **b.** to put in a sequence

5C: Reading/Writing Math Symbols

For use after Lesson 5-4

Study Skill When working on your math homework, use a pencil and have an eraser nearby.

Write each of the following using appropriate mathematical symbols and abbreviations.

1. 3 feet to 1 yard _____

2. 47 and 6 tenths percent _____

3. 37 percent is greater than $\frac{1}{3}$ _____

4. 1 meter to 100 centimeters _____

5. 106 percent _____

6. $\frac{1}{4}$ is less than 26% _____

7. 8 quarts to 2 gallons _____

8. 93 and 32 hundredths percent _____

9. the absolute value of negative 16 _____

10. 78 out of 100 _____

Write each of the following in words.

11. $|-7.3| = 7.3$

_____

12. 30.08%

_____

13. $50\% > \frac{2}{5}$

_____

14. 2 h : 120 min

_____

15. $\frac{55}{100}$

_____

16. $\frac{1}{10} < 12\%$

_____

5D: Visual Vocabulary Practice

High-Use Academic Words

Study Skill When making a sketch, make it simple but make it complete.

Concept List

represent	graph	solve
model	explain	pattern
substitute	calculate	verify

Write the concept that best describes each exercise. Choose from the concept list above

<table>
<tr><td>

1.

35% of 70 is
$0.35 \times 70 = 24.5$

_____
</td><td>

2.

-3 -2 -1 0 1

_____
</td><td>

3.

$5:7$
5 to 7
$\frac{5}{7}$

_____
</td></tr>
<tr><td>

4.

$n + 76 \geq 64$
$n + 76 - 76 \geq 64 - 76$
$n \geq -12$

_____
</td><td>

5.

Sales tax is a percent of a purchase price you must pay when buying certain items. The formula for sales tax is sales tax = tax rate $\times$ purchase price.

_____
</td><td>

6.

If $\frac{t}{18} = \frac{7}{126}$, then $t = 1$.
Check: $1 \times 126 = 7 \times 18$

_____
</td></tr>
<tr><td>

7.

A	B
3	15
6	30
9	45
12	60
15	75

_____
</td><td>

8.

$7a = 161; a$ is either 23 or 26

$7(21) \stackrel{?}{=} 147$ False
$7(23) \stackrel{?}{=} 161$ True

_____
</td><td>

9.

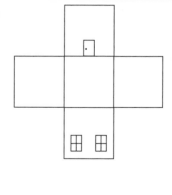

_____
</td></tr>
</table>

5E: Vocabulary Check

Study Skill Strengthen your vocabulary. Use these pages and add cues and summaries by applying the Cornell Notetaking style.

Write the definition for each word or term at the right. To check your work, fold the paper back along the dotted line to see the correct answers.

_____   commission

_____

_____

_____   discount

_____

_____   markup

_____

_____

_____   percent

_____

_____

_____   percent of change

_____

_____

Vocabulary and Study Skills

5E: Vocabulary Check (continued)

For use after Lesson 5-6

Write the vocabulary word or term for each definition. To check your work, fold the paper back along the dotted line to see the correct answers.

pay that is equal to a percent of sales

_____

the difference between the original price and the sale price of an item

_____

the difference between the selling price and the original cost

_____

a ratio that compares a number to 100

_____

the percent a quantity increases or decreases from its original amount

_____

5F: Vocabulary Review

For use with the Chapter Review

Vocabulary and Study Skills

Study Skill When you have to match words and descriptions from two columns, read the list of words and the definitions carefully and completely so you can quickly find the obvious matches. Then do the rest, one at a time. Cross out words and definitions as you use them.

Match the word in Column A with its definition in Column B.

Column A	Column B
1. percent	**A.** difference between the original price and the sale price
2. factor	**B.** equation stating two ratios are equal
3. discount	**C.** whole number that divides into another whole number evenly
4. ratio	**D.** difference between the selling price and the original cost of an item
5. proportion	**E.** comparison of two numbers by division
6. markup	**F.** ratio comparing a number to 100

Match the word in Column A with its definition in Column B.

Column A	Column B
7. mode	**G.** percent a quantity increases or decreases from its original amount
8. equation	**H.** enlarged or reduced drawing of an object
9. commission	**J.** statement that two expressions are equal
10. tip	**K.** number that occurs most often in a data set
11. scale drawing	**L.** percent of sales
12. percent of change	**M.** percent of a bill that you give to a person for providing a service

Practice 6-1

Angle Measures

Solve.

1. If $m\angle A = 23°$, what is the measure of its complement?

_____

2. If $m\angle T = 163°$, what is the measure of its supplement?

_____

3. If a 76° angle is complementary to $\angle Q$, what is the measure of $\angle Q$?

_____

Find the measures of the complement and supplement of each angle.

4. $m\angle A = 41°$ _____

_____

5. $m\angle C = 38.1°$ _____

_____

6. $m\angle S = 87.3°$ _____

_____

7. $m\angle F = 19°$ _____

_____

8. $m\angle R = 76°$ _____

_____

9. $m\angle B = 24.9°$ _____

_____

10. $m\angle N = 62°$ _____

_____

11. In the diagram, $m\angle 1$ is 46°. Find the measures of $\angle 2$, $\angle 3$, and $\angle 4$.

_____

_____

_____

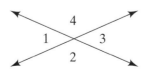

Name _____ Class _____ Date _____

6-1 • Guided Problem Solving

GPS **Student Page 219, Exercise 17:**

Writing in Math Can an angle ever have the same measure as its complement? Explain.

Understand

1. What are you being asked to do?

   _____

   _____

2. What do you have to do to explain your answer?

   _____

   _____

   _____

Plan and Carry Out

3. What is the definition of complementary angles?

   _____

4. If an angle and its complement have the same measure, explain the relationship between the angle and 90°.

   _____

5. Determine the measure of the angle. _____

6. Can an angle ever have the same measure as its complement? _____

Check

7. Explain your answer.

   _____

   _____

Solve Another Problem

8. Can an angle ever have the same measure as its supplement? Explain.

   _____

   _____

Practice 6-2

Area of a Parallelogram

Find the area of each parallelogram.

1.

4 m
4 m

2.
5 cm
23 cm

3.
5 in. 4 in.
8 in.

4.
8 mm
10 mm
10 mm

Find the area of each parallelogram with base *b* and height *h*.

5. $b = 16$ mm, $h = 12$ mm

6. $b = 23$ km, $h = 14$ km

7. $b = 65$ mi, $h = 48$ mi

8. $b = 19$ in., $h = 15$ in.

Solve.

9. The area of a parallelogram is 6 square units. Both the height and the length of the base are whole numbers. What are the possible lengths and heights?

10. The perimeter of a rectangle is 72 m. The width of the rectangle is 16 m. What is the area of the rectangle?

11. The area of a certain rectangle is 288 yd^2. The perimeter is 68 yd. If you double the length and width, what will be the area and perimeter of the new rectangle?

12. If you have 36 ft of fencing, what are the areas of the different rectangles you could enclose with the fencing? Consider only whole-number dimensions.

6-2 • Guided Problem Solving

GPS **Student Page 226, Exercise 22:**

Geography The shape of the state of Tennessee is similar to a
parallelogram. Estimate the area of Tennessee.

Understand

1. What are you being asked to do?

   _____

   _____

2. What shape is Tennessee similar to?

   _____

   _____

3. How do you find the area of a parallelogram?

   _____

   _____

Plan and Carry Out

4. What is the height of Tennessee? _____

5. What is the length of the base of Tennessee? _____

6. Substitute the values into the formula $A = bh$. _____

7. What is the approximate area of Tennessee? _____

Check

8. Is this estimate more or less than the actual area of Tennessee?
   Explain.

   _____

   _____

   _____

Solve Another Problem

9. Tamika's yard is similar to the shape of a parallelogram.
   Estimate the area of Tamika's yard.

   _____

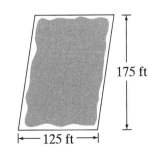

Practice 6-3 .... Area of a Triangle

Find the area of each triangle.

1.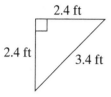
2.4 ft
2.4 ft
3.4 ft

2.
15 ft
201 ft
200 ft

3.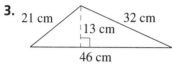
21 cm
32 cm
13 cm
46 cm

4.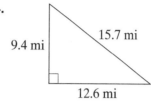
9.4 mi
15.7 mi
12.6 mi

5.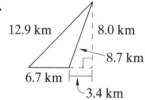
12.9 km
8.0 km
8.7 km
6.7 km
3.4 km

6.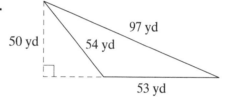
50 yd
97 yd
54 yd
53 yd

Solve.

7. A homeowner plants two flower beds around his garage. What is the total area he will have planted? Round to the nearest tenth.

Garage
Bed 2
Flower Bed 1
5.5 yd
5.5 yd
10 yd

8. The side of an equilateral triangle has a length of 5.4 m. The height of the triangle is approximately 4.7 m. What is the area of this triangle? Round your answer to the nearest tenth.

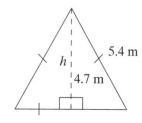
5.4 m
h
4.7 m

6-3 • Guided Problem Solving

Two equilateral triangles with sides of length 6 inches are joined together to form a rhombus. What is the perimeter of the rhombus?

Understand

1. What are you being asked to do? _____

   _____

2. How do you measure the perimeter of a figure?

   _____

3. What is an equilateral triangle? _____

   _____

Plan and Carry Out

4. In the space to the right, draw an equilateral triangle.
   Label all of its sides as 6 in.

5. Draw another equilateral triangle touching the first equilateral
   triangle so that the two triangles form a rhombus.

6. Label the sides of the second triangle as 6 in.

7. Add the lengths of the sides of the rhombus to find the
   perimeter. _____

   _____

Check

8. Count the number of sides that the rhombus has. Multiply this
   number by the length of the sides. Is this number the
   same as your answer? _____

   _____

Solve Another Problem

9. Two right isosceles triangles with legs of 5 in. length and a
   hypotenuse of 7.1 in. are joined together to make a square.
   What is the perimeter of the square?

   _____

Name _____ Class _____ Date _____

Practice 6-4

Areas of Other Figures

Find the area of each trapezoid.

1.
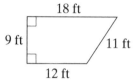
18 ft
9 ft
11 ft
12 ft

2.
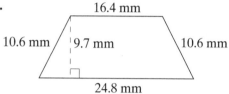
16.4 mm
10.6 mm   9.7 mm   10.6 mm
24.8 mm

3.
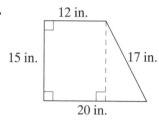
12 in.
15 in.   17 in.
20 in.

_____   _____   _____

4.
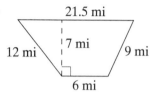
21.5 mi
12 mi   7 mi   9 mi
6 mi

5.
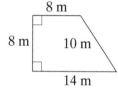
8 m
8 m   10 m
14 m

6.
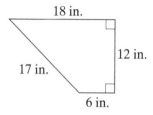
18 in.
17 in.   12 in.
6 in.

_____   _____   _____

Find the area of each irregular figure.

7.
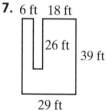
6 ft 18 ft
26 ft   39 ft
29 ft

8.
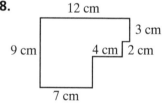
12 cm
9 cm   3 cm
4 cm   2 cm
7 cm

9.

64 m
31 m   58 m

_____   _____   _____

Solve.

10. The flag of Switzerland features a white cross on a red background.

   a. Each of the 12 sides of the cross has a length of 15 cm.
   Find the area of the white cross.   _____

   b. The flag has dimensions 60 cm by 60 cm.
   Find the area of the red region.   _____

11. A trapezoid has an area of 4 square units, and a height of 1 unit. What are
the possible whole-number lengths for the bases?   _____

6-4 • Guided Problem Solving

GPS **Student Page 236, Exercise 17:**

Music A hammer dulcimer is shaped like a trapezoid. The top edge
is 17 in. long, and the bottom edge is 39 in. long. The distance from the
top edge to the bottom edge is 16 in. What is the area of the
dulcimer?

Understand

1. Circle the information you will need to solve the problem.

2. What are you being asked to do?

   _____

   _____

3. How do you find the area of a trapezoid?

   _____

   _____

Plan and Carry Out

4. What is the height of the dulcimer? _____

5. What are the bases of the dulcimer? _____

6. Substitute the values for the bases and
   the height into the formula for area. _____

7. What is the area of the dulcimer? _____

Check

8. Explain how you chose which measurements are the bases.

   _____

   _____

Solve Another Problem

9. Suppose the dulcimer had bases of 20 in. and 36 in. with the same
   height. What would be the area of the dulcimer? How do the areas
   compare? Explain.

   _____

   _____

Name _____ Class _____ Date _____

Practice 6-5 Circumference and Area of a Circle

Find the circumference and area of each circle. Round your answers to the nearest tenth.

1.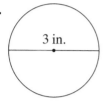
3 in.

_____

2.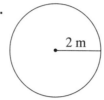
2 m

_____

3.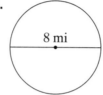
7 ft

_____

4.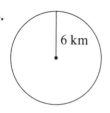
6 km

_____

5.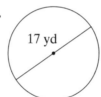
8 mi

_____

6.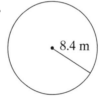
15 in.

_____

7.
15.6 m

_____

8.
17 yd

_____

9.
8.4 m

_____

Estimate the radius of each circle with the given circumference. Round your answer to the nearest tenth.

10. 80 km

_____

11. 92 ft

_____

12. 420 in.

_____

13. In the diagram at the right, the radius of the large circle is 8 in. The radius of each of the smaller circles is 1 in. Find the area of the shaded region to the nearest square unit.

_____

6-5 • Guided Problem Solving

GPS **Student Page 241, Exercise 29:**

Bicycles The front wheel of a high-wheel bicycle from the late 1800s was larger than the rear wheel to increase the bicycle's overall speed. The front wheel measured in height up to 60 in. Find the circumference and area of the front wheel of a high-wheel bicycle.

Understand

1. Circle the information you will need to solve.

2. In the space to the right, draw a sketch of the bicycle that the problem is discussing.

3. What are you being asked to do?

   _____

   _____

Plan and Carry Out

4. What is the diameter of the front wheel? _____

5. What is the radius of the front wheel? _____

6. How do you find the circumference of a circle?

   _____

7. What is the circumference of the front wheel? _____

8. How do you find the area of a circle?

   _____

9. What is the area of the front wheel? _____

Check

10. How do you determine the radius if you know the area and circumference of a circle?

    _____

    _____

Solve Another Problem

11. The diameter of a normal front wheel on a bicycle is 24 in. Find the circumference and area of the front wheel.

    _____

6A: Graphic Organizer

For use before Lesson 6-1

Study Skill Take notes while you study. Writing something down might help you remember it better. Go back and review your notes when you study for quizzes and tests.

Vocabulary and Study Skills

Write your answers.

1. What is the chapter title? _____

2. How many lessons are there in this chapter? _____

3. What is the topic of the Test-Taking Strategies page? _____

4. Complete the graphic organizer below as you work through the chapter.

   • In the center, write the title of the chapter.

   • When you begin a lesson, write the lesson name in a rectangle.

   • When you complete a lesson, write a skill or key concept in a circle linked to that lesson block.

   • When you complete the chapter, use this graphic organizer to help you review.

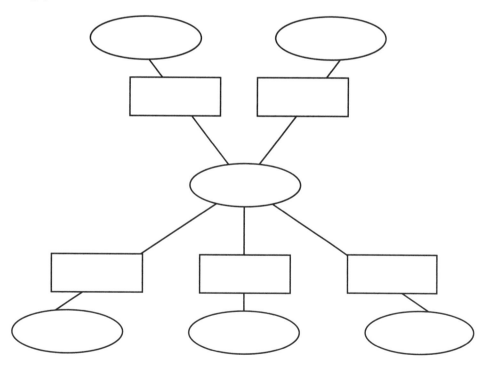

6B: Reading Comprehension

Study Skill Review notes that you have taken in class as soon as possible to clarify any points you missed. Be sure to ask questions if you need extra help.

Here is a circle graph for a monthly household budget. Use the graph to answer the questions that follow.

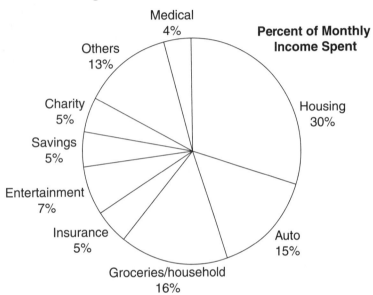

1. On which category was the largest percent of income spent? _____

2. On which category was the smallest percent of income spent? _____

3. Why are the insurance, savings, and charity sectors the same size?

   _____

4. What is the total of the percents listed in the circle graph? _____

5. If the monthly income is $2,400, how much should be spent on an automobile?

   _____

6. How much of a $1,900 monthly income should be saved? _____

7. If $60 is the amount budgeted for entertainment, what is the monthly income?

   _____

8. **High-Use Academic Words** What does it mean to *review*, as mentioned in the study skill?

   a. to put in order   **b.** to study again

6C: Reading/Writing Math Symbols

For use after Lesson 6-3

Study Skill When you take notes, use abbreviations and symbols such as @ (at), # (number), and w/ (with) to save time and reduce writing.

Match the symbol in Column A with its meaning in Column B.

Column A	Column B
1. $\angle ABC$	**A.** the measure of angle ABC
2. $\overline{AB}$	**B.** the length of segment AB
3. $\overleftrightarrow{AB}$	**C.** triangle ABC
4. AB	**D.** segment AB
5. $\overrightarrow{AB}$	**E.** ray starting at A and passing through B
6. $m\angle ABC$	**F.** ray starting at B and passing through A
7. $\overrightarrow{BA}$	**G.** line AB
8. $\triangle ABC$	**H.** angle ABC

Write the meaning of each of the following mathematical statements.

9. $m\angle B = 80°$

_____

10. $BC = 4$

_____

11. $DJ = KL$

_____

12. $m\angle P = m\angle R$

_____

13. $BC = \frac{1}{2}TU$

_____

Find the complement and the supplement of each angle.

14. $m\angle S = 18°$

_____

15. $m\angle T = 81°$

_____

6D: Visual Vocabulary Practice

For use after Lesson 6-5

Study Skill Use Venn Diagrams to understand the relationship between words whose meanings overlap, such as squares, rectangles, and quadrilaterals or real numbers, integers, and counting numbers.

Concept List

obtuse angle	right triangle	adjacent angles
diameter	equilateral triangle	perpendicular lines
midpoint	hexagon	pentagon

Write the concept that best describes each exercise. Choose from the concept list above.

1.

A   B   C   D

Point *B* on $\overline{AC}$

_____

2.

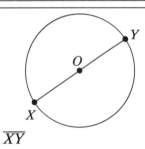

∠*SQT*

_____

3.

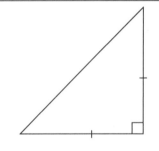

_____

4.

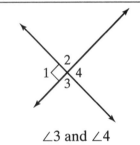

∠3 and ∠4

_____

5.

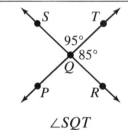

$\overline{XY}$

_____

6.

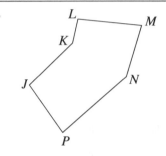

_____

7.

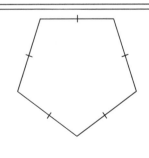

_____

8.

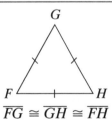

$\overline{FG} \cong \overline{GH} \cong \overline{FH}$

_____

9.

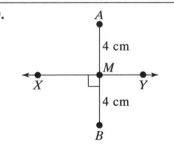

_____

6E: Vocabulary Check

Study Skill Strengthen your vocabulary. Use these pages and add cues and summaries by applying the Cornell Notetaking style.

Write the definition for each word or term at the right. To check your work, fold the paper back along the dotted line to see the correct answers.

_____ polygon

_____

_____

_____ parallel lines

_____

_____ trapezoid

_____

_____

_____ acute angle

_____

_____

_____ circle

_____

_____

Vocabulary and Study Skills

6E: Vocabulary Check (continued)

Write the vocabulary word or term for each definition. To check your work, fold the paper forward along the dotted line to see the correct answers.

a closed figure with sides formed by three or more line segments

_____

lines in the same plane that never intersect

_____

a quadrilateral with exactly one pair of parallel sides

_____

an angle with measure between 0 and 90 degrees

_____

the set of all points in the plane that are the same distance from a given point

_____

6F: Vocabulary Review Puzzle

For use with the Chapter Review

Study Skill Write assignments down; do not rely only on your memory.

Below is a list of clues grouped by the number of letters in the answer. Identify the word each clue represents, and fit each word into the puzzle grid.

Vocabulary and Study Skills

7 letters
- tool used to draw circles and arcs
- polygon with 10 sides
- type of triangle with no congruent sides
- polygon with all sides and angles congruent

8 letters
- point that divides a segment into two segments of equal length
- polygon with 5 sides

9 letters
- sides that have the same length
- type of triangle with at least two sides congruent
- parallelogram with four right angles
- quadrilateral with exactly one pair of parallel sides

11 letters
- triangle with three congruent sides

12 letters
- lines that have exactly one point in common

13 letters
- two angles whose sum is 180°
- two angles whose sum is 90°

3 letters
- part of a circle

5 letters
- angle that measures between 0° and 90°
- formed by two rays with a common endpoint
- segment that has both endpoints on the circle
- flat surface that extends indefinitely in all directions

6 letters
- point of intersection of two sides on an angle or figure
- set of all points in a plane that are the same distance from a given point
- angle that measures between 90° and 180°

Practice 7-1

Three-Dimensional Figures

Describe the base and name the figure.

1.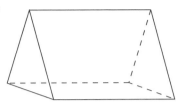

_____

_____

2.

_____

_____

3.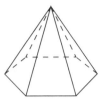

_____

_____

4.

_____

_____

_____

5.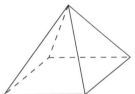

_____

_____

_____

6.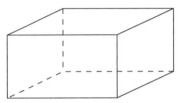

_____

_____

_____

Draw each figure named.

7. a triangular pyramid

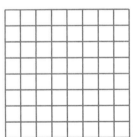

8. a square prism

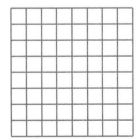

9. a cone

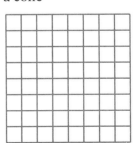

10. a pentagonal pyramid

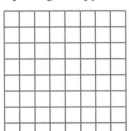

7-1 • Guided Problem Solving

GPS Student Page 255, Exercise 23:

What is the total area of the two bases of the figure at the right?

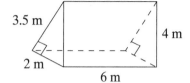

Understand

1. What are you being asked to do?

   _____

2. How many rectangular faces are there?   _____

3. How many triangular faces are there?   _____

Plan and Carry Out

4. Which faces are the bases? Explain how you know.

   _____

5. What is the formula for the area of a triangle?   _____

6. What are the dimensions of the triangular faces?

   _____

7. What is the area of one triangular face?   _____

8. What is the area of all the triangular faces?   _____

Check

9. Did you use the correct information from the diagram to calculate your answer? Explain.

   _____

   _____

Solve Another Problem

10. A rectangular solid has a base 11 in., height 15 in., and a length of 6 in. Find the total area of all faces.

    _____

    _____

Practice 7-2   Surface Areas of Prisms and Cylinders

Find the surface area of each prism.

1.

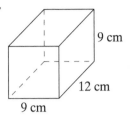

9 cm
12 cm
9 cm

_____

2.

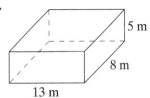

5 m
8 m
13 m

_____

3.

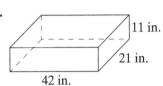

11 in.
21 in.
42 in.

_____

4.

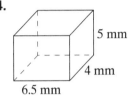

5 mm
4 mm
6.5 mm

_____

Find the surface area of each cylinder. Round to the nearest whole number.

5.

4 ft
21 ft

_____

6.

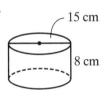

15 cm
8 cm

_____

7.

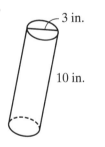

3 in.
10 in.

_____

8.

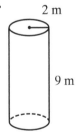

2 m
9 m

_____

Draw a net for each three-dimensional figure.

9.

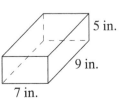

5 in.
9 in.
7 in.

10.

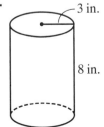

3 in.
8 in.

7-2 • Guided Problem Solving

GPS **Student Page 260, Exercise 22:**

A cosmetics company that makes small cylindrical bars of soap wraps the bars in plastic prior to shipping. Find the surface area of a bar of soap if the diameter is 5 cm and the height is 2 cm. Round to the nearest tenth.

Understand

1. What are you being asked to do?

_____

2. What do you need to do to your final answer?

_____

Plan and Carry Out

3. How do you find the surface area of a cylinder?

_____

_____

4. What formula do you use to find the area of a circular face?

_____

5. What is the total area of the circular faces of a bar of soap?

_____

6. What formula do you use to find the area of the rectangular face?

_____

7. What is the area of the rectangular face of a bar of soap?

_____

8. What is the surface area of a bar of soap? _____

Check

9. Did you find the area of all the surfaces of a bar of soap? Does your answer check?

_____

Solve Another Problem

10. Find the surface area of a cylindrical candle if the diameter is 6 in. and the height is 8 in. Round to the nearest tenth.

_____

Name _____ Class _____ Date _____

Practice 7-3

Volumes of Prisms and Cylinders

Find each volume. Round to the nearest cubic unit.

1. 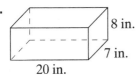 8 in. 7 in. 20 in.

_____

2. 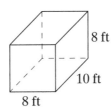 8 ft 10 ft 8 ft

_____

3. 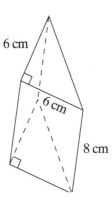 6 cm 6 cm 8 cm

_____

4. 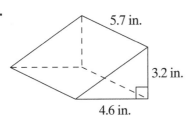 5.7 in. 3.2 in. 4.6 in.

_____

5. 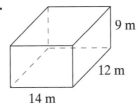 9 m 12 m 14 m

_____

6. 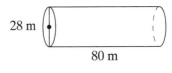 28 m 80 m

_____

7. 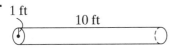 1 ft 10 ft

_____

8. 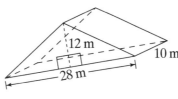 12 m 10 m 28 m

_____

9. 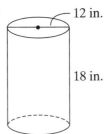 12 in. 18 in.

_____

Find the height of each rectangular prism given the volume, length, and width.

10. $V = 122{,}500 \text{ cm}^3$
$l = 50 \text{ cm}$
$w = 35 \text{ cm}$

_____

11. $V = 22.05 \text{ ft}^3$
$l = 3.5 \text{ ft}$
$w = 4.2 \text{ ft}$

_____

12. $V = 3{,}375 \text{ m}^3$
$l = 15 \text{ m}$
$w = 15 \text{ m}$

_____

7-3 • Guided Problem Solving

GPS Student Page 267, Exercise 21:

Aquariums A large aquarium is built in the shape of a cylinder. The diameter is 203 ft and the height is 25 ft. About how many million gallons of water does this tank hold? (1 gal ≈ 231 in.^{3})

Understand

1. Circle the information you will need to solve.

2. What are you being asked to do?

   _____

   _____

3. What do you need to do to the units in your final answer?

   _____

Plan and Carry Out

4. Write the formula you use to find the volume of a cylinder.

   _____

5. Find the volume of the aquarium in cubic feet.

   _____

6. Convert the answer in Step 5 to cubic inches.

   _____

7. Use the hint to convert the answer in Step 6 to gallons.

   _____

8. About how many million gallons does the tank hold?

   _____

Check

9. Estimate the answer by using 3 for π, 200 ft for the diameter, 2000 in.^{3} ≈ 1 ft^3 and 1 gal ≈ 200 in.^{3} Does your answer make sense?

   _____

   _____

Solve Another Problem

10. The diameter of a tank is 26 cm, and the height is 58 cm. About how many liters of fuel oil can this steel tank hold? (1,000 cm^3 = 1 L)

    _____

Practice 7-4

Describe each cross section.

1.

_____

2.

_____

3.

_____

4.

_____

5. A block of cheese has the shape of a cylinder. Russell wants to cut the block vertically. Sierra wants to cut the block horizontally. Draw and describe the shape of each cross section.

   a.

   Vertical Slice

   _____

   b.

   Horizontal Slice

   _____

6. A carpenter has a block of wood in the shape of a trapezoidal prism. Draw lines on each prism to show how the carpenter should slice the wood to produce each type of cross section.

   a. **trapezoid**

   b. **square**

   c. **rectangle**

   d. **triangle**

Course 2 Lesson 7-4 **227**

7-4 • Guided Problem Solving

GPS **Student Page 274, Exercise 16:**

A three-dimensional figure has a rectangular vertical cross section and a horizontal cross section in the shape of a hexagon.

vertical cross section

horizontal cross section

What is the three-dimensional figure?

Understand

1. Circle the information you will need to solve this problem.

2. What are you being asked to do?

_____

_____

Plan and Carry Out

3. Is the three-dimensional figure you will identify going to be a prism or a pyramid?

_____

4. What shape will the face(s) of the figure have?

_____

5. Draw and identify the three-dimensional figure.

_____

Check

6. Draw the two cross sections given in the problem on your figure to check your answer.

Solve Another Problem

7. A three-dimensional figure has a trapezoidal vertical cross section and a horizontal cross section in the shape of a rectangle.

vertical cross section

horizontal cross section

What is the three-dimensional figure?

_____

7A: Graphic Organizer

For use before Lesson 7-1

Vocabulary and Study Skills

Study Skill Take a few minutes to relax before and after studying. Your mind will absorb and retain more information if you alternate studying with brief rest intervals.

Write your answers.

1. What is the chapter title? _____

2. How many lessons are there in this chapter? _____

3. What is the topic of the Test-Taking Strategies page? _____

4. Complete the graphic organizer below as you work through the chapter.

   • In the center, write the title of the chapter.

   • When you begin a lesson, write the lesson name in a rectangle.

   • When you complete a lesson, write a skill or key concept in a circle linked to that lesson block.

   • When you complete the chapter, use this graphic organizer to help you review.

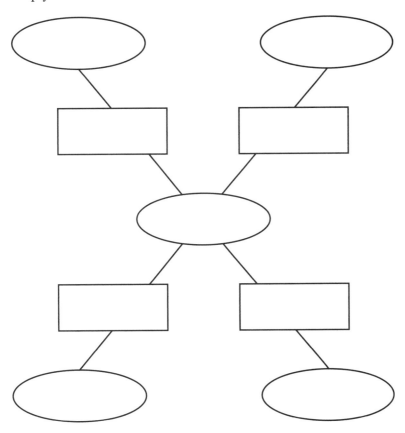

7B: Reading Comprehension

Study Skill Learning to read for detail takes practice. As you read your notes, underline or highlight important information.

Read the paragraph and answer the questions.

> The Grand Canyon was formed by the Colorado River in Arizona. It is estimated to be nearly 10 million years old. With a length of 277 miles, the Grand Canyon is nearly 18 miles wide at its widest point and one mile deep in some places. Arizona, called the Grand Canyon State, has a total land area of approximately 113,000 square miles.

1. What is the paragraph about?

_____

2. How old is the Grand Canyon?

_____

3. What dimensions are given for the Grand Canyon?

_____

4. Use these dimensions to calculate the approximate area of the bottom of the Grand Canyon.

_____

5. What percent of the land area in Arizona is occupied by the Grand Canyon?

_____

6. Why is the area determined in Exercise 4 a maximum area?

_____

_____

7. What is the approximate volume of the Grand Canyon?

_____

8. **High-Use Academic Words** In Exercise 4, what does it mean to *calculate?*

  a. to determine by mathematical processes   **b.** to show that you recognize something

7C: Reading/Writing Math Symbols

For use after Lesson 7-4

Study Skill After completing an assignment, take a break. Then, come back and check your work.

State whether each of the following units represents length, area or volume.

1. cm^2 _____

2. $in.^3$ _____

3. mi _____

4. ft^2 _____

5. km _____

6. mm^3 _____

State whether each expression can be used to calculate length, area, or volume and to what shapes they apply.

7. $\frac{1}{2}bh$ _____

8. lwh _____

9. bh _____

10. πd _____

11. πr^2 _____

12. S^2 _____

13. $\frac{1}{2}h(b_1 + b_2)$ _____

14. $\pi r^2 h$ _____

15. $2\pi r$ _____

7D: Visual Vocabulary Practice

For use after Lesson 7-4

Study Skill When interpreting an illustration, look for the most specific concept represented.

Concept List

circumference	base	cone
Pythagorean Theorem	perfect square	edges
vertices	prism	pyramid

Write the concept that best describes each exercise. Choose from the concept list above.

1. $AB^2 = 6^2 + 8^2$ $AB^2 = 36 + 64 = 100$ $AB = \sqrt{100} = 10$ 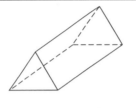6 cm, 8 cm _____	**2.** 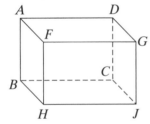 _____	**3.** 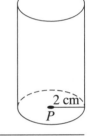Circle P is one for this cylinder. 2 cm P _____
4. 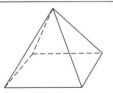 $\overline{AB}$ and $\overline{CJ}$ are examples _____	**5.** 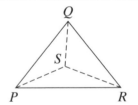 _____	**6.** 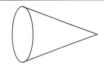 There are four of these in this three-dimensional figure. _____
7. _____	**8.** 576, since $24^2 = 576$. _____	**9.** 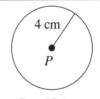4 cm P $C \approx 25.1$ cm _____

7E: Vocabulary Check

For use after Lesson 7-4

Study Skill Strengthen your vocabulary. Use these pages and add cues and summaries by applying the Cornell Notetaking style.

Write the definition for each word or term at the right. To check your work, fold the paper back along the dotted line to see the correct answers.

cross section

face

surface area

volume

prism

Vocabulary and Study Skills

7E: Vocabulary Check (continued) · · · · · · · · · · · · · · · · · For use after Lesson 7-4

Write the vocabulary word or term for each definition. To check your work, fold the paper forward along the dotted line to see the correct answers.

two-dimensional shape that is seen
after slicing through a 3-dimensional
object

_____

a flat surface of a three-dimensional
figure that is shaped
like a polygon

_____

sum of the areas of the faces

_____

the number of cubic units needed
to fill the space inside a three-
dimensional figure

_____

a three-dimensional figure with
two parallel and congruent
polygonal faces, called bases

_____

7F: Vocabulary Review

Study Skill Participating in class discussions will help you remember new material. Do not be afraid to express your thoughts when your teacher asks for questions, answers, or discussion.

Circle the word that best completes the sentence.

1. The longest side of a right triangle is the (*leg, hypotenuse*).

2. (*Parallel, Perpendicular*) lines lie in the same plane and do not intersect.

3. A (*solution, statement*) is a value of a variable that makes an equation true.

4. Figures that are the same size and shape are (*similar, congruent*).

5. (*Complementary, Supplementary*) angles are two angles whose sum is 90°.

6. A (*circle, sphere*) is the set of all points in space that are the same distance from a center point.

7. The perimeter of a circle is the (*circumference, circumcenter*).

8. The (*area, volume*) of a figure is the number of square units it encloses.

9. A(n) (*isosceles, scalene*) triangle has no congruent sides.

10. A (*rhombus, square*) is a parallelogram with four right angles and four congruent sides.

11. A number that is the square of an integer is a (*perfect square, square root*).

12. A (*pyramid, prism*) is a three-dimensional figure with triangular faces that meet at one point.

13. A speed limit of 65 mi/h is an example of a (*ratio, rate*).

14. A (*cone, cylinder*) has two congruent parallel bases that are circles.

Name _____ Class _____ Date _____

Practice 8-1

You want to survey students in your school about their exercise habits. Tell whether the situations described in Exercises 1 and 2 are likely to give a random sample of the population. Explain.

1. You select every tenth student on an alphabetical list of the students in your school. You survey the selected students in their first-period classes.

   _____

   _____

2. At lunchtime you stand by a vending machine. You survey every student who buys something from the vending machine.

   _____

   _____

Is each question *biased* or *fair*? Rewrite biased questions as fair questions.

3. Do you think bike helmets should be mandatory for all bike riders?

   _____

4. Do you prefer the natural beauty of hardwood floors in your home?

   _____

5. Do you exercise regularly?

   _____

6. Do you eat at least the recommended number of servings of fruits and vegetables to ensure a healthy and long life?

   _____

7. Do you prefer the look and feel of thick lush carpeting in your living room?

   _____

8. Do you take a daily multiple vitamin to supplement your diet?

   _____

9. Do you read the newspaper to be informed about world events?

   _____

10. Do you feel that the TV news is a sensational portrayal of life's problems?

   _____

8-1 • Guided Problem Solving

GPS **Student Page 285, Exercise 19:**

Parks Suppose you are gathering information about visitors to Yosemite National Park. You survey every tenth person entering the park. Would you get a random sample of visitors? Explain.

Understand

1. What is a random sample?

   _____

   _____

2. What are you being asked to do?

   _____

   _____

Plan and Carry Out

3. What is the population you are surveying?

   _____

4. Does every person in the population
   have an equal chance of being surveyed? _____

5. Is this a random sample? Why or why not? _____

   _____

Check

6. How else could you randomly survey the people at Yosemite National Park?

   _____

   _____

Solve Another Problem

7. You want to survey the people at the local pool about the food served in the snack shack. You decide to walk around the kiddy pool and survey parents. Is this a random sample? Why or why not?

   _____

   _____

   _____

Practice 8-2

Estimating Population Size

Workers at a state park caught, tagged, and set free the species shown at the right. Later that same year, the workers caught the number of animals shown in the table below and counted the tagged animals. Use a proportion to estimate the park population of each species.

Tagged Animals	
Bears	12
Squirrels	50
Raccoons	23
Rabbits	42
Trout	46
Skunks	21

	Caught	Counted Tagged	Estimated Population
1. Bears	30	9	
2. Squirrels	1,102	28	
3. Raccoons	412	10	
4. Rabbits	210	2	
5. Trout	318	25	
6. Skunks	45	6	

A park ranger tags 100 animals. Use a proportion to estimate the total population for each sample.

7. 23 out of 100 animals are tagged

_____

8. 12 out of 75 animals are tagged

_____

9. 8 out of 116 animals are tagged

_____

10. 5 out of 63 animals are tagged

_____

11. 4 out of 83 animals are tagged

_____

12. 3 out of 121 animals are tagged

_____

13. 83 out of 125 animals are tagged

_____

14. 7 out of 165 animals are tagged

_____

Use a proportion to estimate each animal population.

15. Total ducks counted: 1,100
Marked ducks counted: 257
Total marked ducks: 960

_____

16. Total alligators counted: 310
Marked alligators counted: 16
Total marked alligators: 90

_____

8-2 • Guided Problem Solving

Student Page 288, Exercise 19:

Sharks A biologist is studying the shark population off the Florida coast. He captures, tags, and sets free 38 sharks. A week later, 8 out of 25 sharks captured have tags. He uses the proportion $\frac{25}{8} = \frac{38}{x}$ to estimate that the population is about 12.

  a. Error Analysis Find the error in the biologist's proportion.

  b. Estimate the shark population.

Understand

1. What are you being asked to do?

_____

Plan and Carry Out

2. If x represents all the sharks off the coast of Florida, write the ratio of the sharks the biologist originally tagged to the number of all the sharks off the coast of Florida. _____

3. How many sharks did the biologist capture the second time? How many were tagged? _____

4. Write a ratio comparing the sharks the biologist found tagged and the number that were captured the second time. _____

5. Set the ratios from Steps 2 and 4 equal to form the correct proportion. _____

6. What is wrong with the biologist's proportion? _____

7. Solve this proportion to find the correct estimate. _____

Check

8. Explain why the biologist should have known the estimate was wrong.

_____

_____

Solve Another Problem

9. A ranger traps, tags, and releases 32 jackrabbits. Later she captures 12 jackrabbits, of which 4 are tagged. The ranger estimates that there are 96 jackrabbits in the area. Write a proportion and check the ranger's estimate. Is she correct?

_____

Name_____ Class_____ Date_____

Practice 8-3

The tables below show the number of hours a random sample of park visitors spent at the park during the months of January and June. Use the samples to make an inference about each measure. Support your answer.

Random Sample of Hours - January									
2	2	3	1	4	2	1	7	4	1
3	2	4	5	6	3	3	2	4	3

Random Sample of Hours - June									
2	3	4	2	5	4	9	1	5	3
1	8	2	6	4	3	7	6	8	5

1. the mean number of hours visitors spent in the park in January _____

_____

2. the mean number of hours visitors spent in the park in June _____

_____

_____

3. Compare the mean number of hours visitors spent in the park in January to the mean number of hours visitors spent in the park in June.

_____

_____

_____

About 450 people visit a local travel expo. A local travel agency owner surveys 3 random samples of 20 people each about their favorite vacation destinations. The table at the right shows the results.

	Sample 1	Sample 2	Sample 3
Beach	8	7	4
Mountains	9	6	10
City	3	7	6

4. For each sample, estimate how many people prefer to vacation in the mountains.

_____

5. Describe the variation in the predictions. _____

6. Make an inference about the number of people who will prefer to vacation in the mountains.

_____

_____

8-3 • Guided Problem Solving

GPS **Student Page 295, Exercise 13:**

Reasoning A government inspector takes 5 random samples of the same size from a shipment of eggs. She determines the mean weight of a dozen eggs in each sample. What can the inspector conclude if the mean weights of the samples are very close to each other?

Understand

1. What are you being asked to do? _____

_____

2. How will you find the answer? _____

_____

Plan and Carry Out

3. How do you find the mean weight of one sample of eggs? _____

_____

4. What does the mean tell you about a sample? _____

_____

5. What can you tell by comparing the means of all the samples? _____

_____

6. What can you conclude if the mean weights of all the samples are
   very close to each other?

_____

_____

Check

7. How can you be sure your answer is correct? _____

_____

Solve Another Problem

8. A poll taker interviews 10 random samples of 20 people each about
   the number of minutes they spend exercising each day. What can the
   poll taker conclude if the mean numbers of minutes spent exercising
   per day are very far apart? _____

_____

Practice 8-4

Data Variability

1. A biologist collects data about beard length on wild turkeys. Compare the IQRs of the data sets, and use the comparison to make an inference.

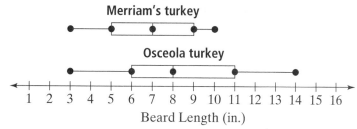

Merriam's turkey

Osceola turkey

Beard Length (in.)

IQR for Merriam's wild turkey: ☐   IQR for Osceola wild turkey: ☐

What can you infer? Explain your reasoning.

_____

_____

_____

The line plot at the right shows the number of homeruns hit by players in a homerun derby.

2. Calculate the mean of each data set.

   Teens: ☐

   Adults: ☐

3. Determine the MAD for each data set.

   Teens: ☐

   Adults: ☐

4. What number n multiplied by the MAD equals the difference between the means?

   MAD: ☐

5. What does this number tell you about the overlap of the data sets?

Homeruns		
Teens		Adults
✗ ✗	1	✗
✗ ✗	2	
✗	3	✗ ✗
✗	4	✗ ✗ ✗
✗ ✗	5	
	6	
✗	7	✗ ✗
	8	✗
	9	✗
✗	10	

8-4 • Guided Problem Solving

GPS Student Page 300, Exercise 12:

Reasoning Biologists capture a spotted hyena that weighs 142 pounds.
Can you tell from its weight whether it is male or female? Explain.

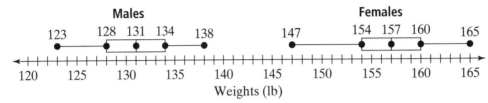

Understand

1. What are you being asked to do?

   _____

2. What will you use to find the answer? _____

Plan and Carry Out

3. What is the maximum weight given for male spotted hyenas? _____

4. What is the minimum weight given for female spotted hyenas? _____

5. Does the weight of 142 pounds fit into either the male or female range? _____

6. Can you tell whether the spotted hyena is male or female based on its weight? Explain.

   _____

   _____

   _____

Check

7. Plot the weight 142 on the number line above.

Solve Another Problem

8. The box-plot below shows the scores of students. Based on the plot,
   can you tell if a student who scored 1,360 took the Study Skills course?

   _____

   _____

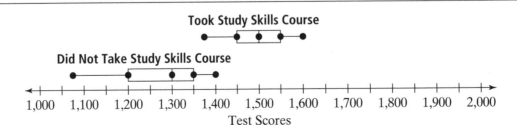

8A: Graphic Organizer

Study Skill As your teacher presents new material in the chapter, keep a paper and pencil handy to write down notes and questions. If you miss class, borrow a classmate's notes so you will not fall behind.

Write your answers.

1. What is the chapter title? _____

2. How many lessons are there in this chapter? _____

3. What is the topic of the Test-Taking Strategies page? _____

4. Complete the graphic organizer below as you work through the chapter.
   - In the center, write the title of the chapter.
   - When you begin a lesson, write the lesson name in a rectangle.
   - When you complete a lesson, write a skill or key concept in a circle linked to that lesson block.
   - When you complete the chapter, use this graphic organizer to help you review.

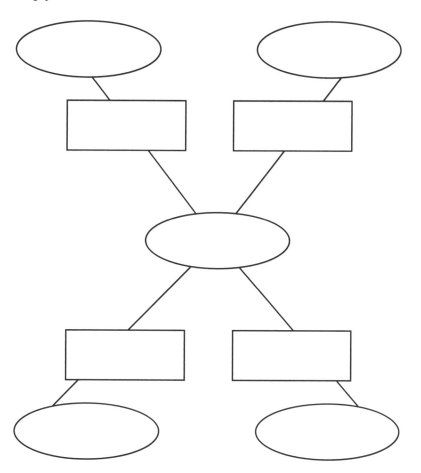

8B: Reading Comprehension

Study Skill Take short breaks between assignments.

Read the paragraph and answer the questions.

In 1945, the first electronic computer was built. ENIAC, which stands for Electronic Numerical Integrator and Calculator, was able to do 5,000 additions per second. Current computers are capable of doing 100,000 times as many additions per second. ENIAC weighed approximately 30 tons and had a length of 40 feet and a width of 45 feet. Present-day computer notebooks weigh about 3 pounds. Unlike modern computers, which use microprocessors composed of thousands or millions of transistors, ENIAC used vacuum tubes to process data. It had about 18,000 tubes, each the size of a small light bulb.

1. What does the acronym ENIAC stand for?

_____

2. How many years ago was ENIAC built?

_____

3. How many additions could ENIAC perform per second?

_____

4. How many additions per second do current computers perform?

_____

5. How much area did ENIAC cover?

_____

6. How many pounds did ENIAC weigh?

_____

7. How many times more does ENIAC weigh than today's notebook computers?

_____

8. What do today's modern computers use to process data?

_____

9. **High-Use Academic Words** In Exercise 1, what does the word *acronym* mean?

   a. a certain way in which something appears

   b. a word formed from the first letters of several other words

8C: Reading/Writing Math Symbols

For use after Lesson 8-4

Study Skill Make a realistic study schedule. Plan ahead when your teacher assigns a long-term project.

Some mathematical symbols have multiple meanings. Explain the meaning of the bar (−) in each of the following.

1. $2.\overline{3}$

_____

2. $11 - 15$

_____

3. $\overline{GH}$

_____

4. $3 + (-7)$

_____

5. $\frac{1}{5}$

_____

_____

The bar (−) takes on different meanings when used with other symbols. Explain the meaning of each symbol below.

6. $=$ _____

7. $\leq$ _____

8. $\cong$ _____

9. $\stackrel{?}{=}$ _____

10. $\neq$ _____

When they are vertical, the bars also take on different meanings. Explain the meaning of these symbols.

11. $| \; |$, as in $|-3| = 3$

_____

12. $\|$, as in $m \parallel n$

_____

Vocabulary and Study Skills

8D: Visual Vocabulary Practice

For use after Lesson 8-4

Study Skill When interpreting an illustration, notice the information that is given and also notice what is not given. Do not make assumptions.

Concept List

biased question	proportion	variability
frequency table	line plot	population
sample	interquartile range (IQR)	inference

Write the concept that best describes each exercise. Choose from the concept list above.

1. Measure of how much the data is spread out.	**2.** **Number of Sports Played by Students**	**3.** Sandy conducted a survey at her college. She chose a random sample from all freshmen and asked how much time they study each week. The freshmen class represents this for the survey.

2.

Number of Sports Played by Students

Sports	Tally	Frequency
0	⊬⊦⊦	5
1	||	2
2	|||	3
3	⊬⊦⊦ ||	7

4. A prediction or conclusion	**5.** **Books Read Last Month**	**6.** Used to estimate population size.

5.

Books Read Last Month

```
       ×       ×
       ×       ×
       ×       ×
       ×       ×
       ×   ×   ×
   ×   ×   ×   ×
  ─────────────────
   0   1   2   3
```

7. "Do you prefer lovable dogs or lazy cats?"	**8.** Difference between upper and lower quartiles	**9.** Derrick conducted a survey using the customers at a local ice cream shop. Derrick chose every 5th and 8th customer entering the shop to represent this.

Vocabulary and Study Skills

8E: Vocabulary Check

Study Skill Strengthen your vocabulary. Use these pages and add cues and summaries by applying the Cornell Notetaking style.

Write the definition for each word or term at the right. To check your work, fold the paper back along the dotted line to see the correct answers.

Vocabulary and Study Skills

_____   biased question

_____
_____

_____   population

_____
_____

_____   mean absolute
_____   deviation
_____   (MAD)

_____   inference

_____
_____

_____   random sample

_____
_____

8E: Vocabulary Check (continued)

Write the vocabulary word or term for each definition. To check your work, fold the paper forward along the dotted line to see the correct answers.

a question that makes an unjustified
assumption or makes one answer
appear better than the other

_____

a group of objects or people

_____

measures the average
distance between the
mean and the data values

_____

predictions or
conclusions based on
data or reasoning

_____

a sample where each member of
the population has an equal
chance of being selected

_____

8F: Vocabulary Review

Study Skill Take notes while you study. Use a highlighter to emphasize important material in your notes.

Circle the term that correctly completes each sentence.

1. A flip that creates symmetry is a (*translation, reflection*).

2. The first number in an ordered pair is the (*x, y*) coordinate.

3. Lines in a coordinate plane that are parallel to the *y*-axis are (*horizontal, vertical*).

4. A (*line plot, frequency table*) uses a number line with "x" marks to represent each data item.

5. You can use a (*bar, circle*) graph to easily compare amounts.

6. The (*mean, median*) is the middle number in a data set when the values are written in order from least to greatest.

7. The (*mode, range*) of a data set is the difference between the greatest and least data values.

8. A (*line graph, box plot*) can be used to investigate the variability in a set of data.

9. A sequence is (*arithmetic, geometric*) if each term is found by adding the same number to the previous term.

10. (*Principal, Interest*) is the amount of money borrowed or deposited.

11. The (*area, surface area*) of a prism is the sum of the areas of the faces.

12. (*Circumference, Area*) is the distance around a circle.

13. The opposite of squaring a number is finding its (*square root, perfect square*).

14. The (*slope, bisector*) of a line segment is a line, segment, or ray, that goes through the midpoint of the segment.

Practice 9-1

Probability

You spin a spinner numbered 1 through 10. Each outcome is equally likely. Find the probabilities below as a fraction, decimal, and percent.

1. $P(9)$

2. $P(\text{even})$

3. $P(\text{number greater than 0})$

4. $P(\text{multiple of 4})$

_____ _____ _____ _____

There are eight blue marbles, nine orange marbles, and six yellow marbles in a bag. You draw one marble at random. Find each probability.

5. $P(\text{blue marble})$ _____

6. $P(\text{yellow marble})$ _____

7. What marble could you add or remove so that the probability of drawing a blue marble is $\frac{1}{3}$?

_____

A box contains 12 slips of paper as shown. Each slip of paper is equally likely to be drawn. Find each probability.

red	blue	yellow	blue
yellow	red	blue	red
red	red	red	yellow

8. $P(\text{red})$

9. $P(\text{blue})$

10. $P(\text{yellow})$

_____ _____ _____

11. $P(\text{red or blue})$

12. $P(\text{red or yellow})$

13. $P(\text{blue or yellow})$

_____ _____ _____

14. $P(\text{not red})$

15. $P(\text{not blue})$

16. $P(\text{not yellow})$

_____ _____ _____

You select a letter randomly from a bag containing the letters S, P, I, N, N, E, and R. Find the odds in favor of each outcome.

17. selecting an N

18. selecting an S

_____ _____

9-1 • Guided Problem Solving

GPS **Student Page 311, Exercise 30:**

a. Suppose $P(E) = 0.3$. Find $P(\text{not } E)$.

b. Suppose $P(\text{not } E) = 65\%$. Find $P(E)$.

Understand

1. What is the relationship between E and not E?

_____

2. What is the sum of the probability of an event
and the probability of the event's complement? _____

3. What is the difference between part (a) and part (b)?

_____

_____

Plan and Carry Out

4. Write an equation for part (a) using the definition of a complement.

_____

5. Solve the equation for $P(\text{not } E)$. _____

6. Write 65% as a decimal. _____

7. Write an equation for part (b) using the definition of a complement.

_____

8. Solve the equation for $P(E)$. _____

Check

9. How could you use a sum to check your answers?

_____

_____

Solve Another Problem

10. Suppose $P(E) = \frac{4}{5}$. Find $P(\text{not } E)$.

_____

Practice 9-2

Suppose you observe the color of socks worn by students in your class: 12 have white, 4 have black, 3 have blue, and 1 has red. Find each experimental probability as a fraction in simplest form.

1. P(white) _____

2. P(red) _____

3. P(blue) _____

4. P(black) _____

5. P(yellow) _____

6. P(black or red) _____

Use the data in the table at the right for Exercises 7–12. Find each experimental probability as a percent.

7. P(fruit) _____

8. P(granola) _____

9. P(pretzels) _____

10. P(carrots) _____

11. P(not fruit) _____

12. P(granola or chips) _____

13. Do an experiment to find the probability that a word chosen randomly in a book is the word *the*. How many words did you look at to find P(the)? What is P(the)?

_____

Favorite Snack Survey Results

Snack	Number of Students
Fruit	8
Granola	2
Pretzels	3
Chips	7
Carrots	5

14. Suppose the following is the result of tossing a coin 5 times:

heads, tails, heads, tails, heads

What is the experimental probability for heads?

_____

Solve.

15. The probability that a twelve-year-old has a brother or sister is 25%. Suppose you survey 300 twelve-year-olds. About how many do you think will have a brother or sister?

_____

16. a. A quality control inspector found flaws in 13 out of 150 sweaters. Find the probability that a sweater has a flaw. Round to the nearest tenth of a percent.

_____

b. Suppose the company produces 500 sweaters a day. How many will not have flaws?

_____

c. Suppose the company produces 600 sweaters a day. How many will have flaws?

_____

9-2 • Guided Problem Solving

GPS **Student Page 315, Exercise 14:**

a. **Science** The probability that a male human is colorblind is 8%. Suppose you interview 1,000 males. About how many would you expect to be colorblind?

b. **Reasoning** Will you always get the same number? Explain.

Understand

1. What does it mean to be colorblind?

_____

2. What are you being asked to do in part (a)?

_____

_____

Plan and Carry Out

3. Find 8% of 1,000. _____

4. How many males out of 1,000 would you expect to be colorblind?

_____

5. Will you always get exactly this number? Explain.

_____

_____

_____

Check

6. How could you find the answer another way?

_____

Solve Another Problem

7. The probability of a person being left-handed is about 11%. Suppose you interview 500 people. About how many would you expect to be left-handed?

_____

Practice 9-3

Make a table to show the sample space and find the number of outcomes. Then find the probability.

1. A theater uses a letter to show which row a seat is in, and a number to show the column. If there are eight rows and ten columns, what is the probability that you select a seat at random that is in column 1? _____

Make a tree diagram. Then find the probability.

2. A coin is tossed three times.
   a. Make a tree diagram that shows all the possible outcomes of how the coin will land.
   b. Find the probability that the coin will land heads up all three times or tails up all three times. _____

Use the counting principle.

3. A pizza company makes pizza in three different sizes: small, medium, and large. There are four possible toppings: pepperoni, sausage, green pepper, and mushroom. How many different kinds of pizza with one topping are available? _____

4. You can choose from three types of sandwiches for lunch and three types of juice. How many possible lunch combinations of sandwich and juice can you have? _____

Susan has red, blue, and yellow sweaters. Joanne has green, red, and white sweaters. Diane's sweaters are red, blue, and mauve. Each girl has only one sweater of each color and will pick a sweater to wear at random. Find each probability.

5. *P*(each girl chooses a different color)

_____

6. *P*(each girl chooses the same color)

_____

7. *P*(two girls choose the same color, and the third chooses a different color)

_____

8. *P*(each girl chooses a red sweater)

_____

9-3 • Guided Problem Solving

GPS **Student Page 323, Exercise 23:**

a. **Clothes** Ardell has four suit jackets (white, blue, green, and tan) and four dress shirts in the same colors. How many different jacket/shirt outfits does Ardell have?

b. Suppose he grabs a suit jacket and a dress shirt without looking. What is the probability that they will *not* be the same color?

Understand

1. Circle the information you will need to solve.

2. How do you find probability?

_____

_____

Plan and Carry Out

3. How many different suit jackets are there? _____

4. How many different dress shirts are there? _____

5. Using the counting principle, how many different jacket/shirt outfits does Ardell have? _____

6. How many same color jacket/shirt outfits does Ardell have? _____

7. How many different color jacket/shirt outfits does Ardell have? _____

8. What is the probability that they will *not* be the same color? _____

Check

9. How else could you find the total number of jacket/shirt outfits?

_____

Solve Another Problem

10. a. Joseph has three pairs of shoes (white, brown, and black) and four pairs of socks (white, brown, black, and blue). How many sock/shoe pairs are there? _____

b. If Joseph selects a pair of shoes and a pair of socks without looking, what is the probability they will be the same color?

_____

Practice 9-4   **Compound Events**

Each letter in the word MASSACHUSETTS is written on a card. The cards are placed in a basket. Find each probability.

1. What is the probability of selecting two S's if the first card is replaced before selecting the second card?

_____

2. What is the probability of selecting two S's if the first card is not replaced before selecting the second card?

_____

You roll a fair number cube. Find each probability.

3. $P(3, \text{then } 5)$

_____

4. $P(2, \text{then } 2)$

_____

5. $P(5, \text{then } 4, \text{then } 6)$

_____

6. $P(6, \text{then } 0)$

_____

Four girls and eight boys are running for president or vice president of the Student Council. Find each probability.

7. Find the probability that two boys are elected.

_____

8. Find the probability that two girls are elected.

_____

9. Find the probability that the president is a boy and the vice president is a girl.

_____

10. Find the probability that the president is a girl and the vice president is a boy.

_____

A box contains ten balls, numbered 1 through 10. Marisha draws a ball. She records its number and then returns it to the bag. Then Penney draws a ball. Find each probability.

11. $P(9, \text{then } 3)$

_____

12. $P(\text{even, then odd})$

_____

13. $P(\text{odd, then } 2)$

_____

14. $P(\text{the sum of the numbers is } 25)$

_____

15. $P(\text{prime, then composite})$

_____

16. $P(\text{a factor of } 8, \text{then a multiple of } 2)$

_____

9-4 • Guided Problem Solving

GPS **Student Page 330, Exercise 26:**

Events with no outcomes in common are called *disjoint events* or *mutually exclusive events*. To find the probability of mutually exclusive events, add the probabilities of the individual events. Suppose you select a number from 21 to 30 at random. What is the probability of selecting a number that is even or prime?

Understand

1. What are disjoint or mutually exclusive events?

   _____

2. What are you being asked to do?

   _____

   _____

3. Why are selecting an even and selecting a prime number between 21 and 30 disjoint events?

   _____

Plan and Carry Out

4. How many numbers are there from 21 to 30? (Remember to include 21 and 30.) _____

5. List all the even numbers between 21 and 30. How many are there? _____

6. What is the probability of choosing an even number between 21 and 30? _____

7. List all the prime numbers between 21 and 30. How many are there? _____

8. What is the probability of choosing a prime number between 21 and 30? _____

9. What is the probability of choosing an even or prime number between 21 and 30? _____

Check

10. Write your answer as a fraction, decimal, and percent. _____

Solve Another Problem

11. Suppose you roll a number cube. What is the probability that you roll a number less than 3 or a number greater than or equal to 5?

Name _____ Class _____ Date _____

Practice 9-5

1. The table shows the fraction of different types of pencils in Eva's pencil box.

Type	Fraction
Plain	$\frac{1}{5}$
Glitter	$\frac{2}{5}$
Message	$\frac{2}{5}$

  a. Design a simulation that can be used to estimate the probability that Eva will need to pick more than 3 randomly chosen glitter pencils from the pencil box before getting a plain pencil.

_____

_____

_____

_____

_____

  b. Perform 20 trials of the simulation. Then estimate the probability.

_____

2. A grocery store includes one token with every purchase. Half of the tokens are for free merchandise, and the other half are for prizes.

  a. Design a simulation that can be used to estimate the probability that a customer will need to make at least 2 purchases to receive a token for a prize.

_____

_____

_____

_____

  b. Perform 20 trials of the simulation. Then estimate the probability.

_____

In a satisfaction survey, 11% of a tour guide's customers said that the tour was too short. However, 48% said the tour was great. Estimate the probability that the guide will have to read at least 5 surveys to find one that said the tour was too short. Then estimate the probability that the guide will have to read at least 5 surveys to find one saying the tour was great.

Tour Guide Surveys			
02	19	24	61
32	43	30	17
18	68	55	11
08	90	72	03
49	63	80	52
12	27	34	70
20	49	03	66
52	78	83	54
60	48	52	77
13	61	27	91

3. Probability of reading at least 5 surveys to find one that said the tour was too short: _____

4. Probability of reading at least 5 surveys to find one that said the tour was great: _____

Name _____ Class _____ Date _____

9-5 • Guided Problem Solving

GPS Student Page 338, Exercise 9:

Consumer Math A restaurant gives out a scratch-off ticket with each purchase of a $5 meal deal. Two thirds of the tickets are winners. Design a simulation and perform 20 trials to estimate the probability that a customer will need to spend at least $15 to get a winning ticket.

Understand

1. What are you being asked to do?

   _____

   _____

2. What will you use to find the answer?

   _____

   _____

Plan and Carry Out

3. What fraction shows the amount of tickets that win? _____

4. What simulation tool would work best with this fraction? _____

5. How many meals will $15 buy? _____

6. Let 1 and 2 represent winning tickets. Perform 20 trials. Complete the frequency table. _____

7. What is the probability that a customer will need to spend at least $15 to get a winning ticket?

   _____

Meals Bought to Get Winning Ticket	Frequency
1	
2	
3 or more	

Check

8. How can you check your answer?

   _____

Solve Another Problem

9. A sporting goods store holds a drawing for new merchandise. Each purchase of $20 or more gives a customer one entry into the drawing. Three fourths of the entries win a prize. Design a simulation and perform 20 trials to estimate the probability that a customer will need to spend at least $60 to win a prize.

   _____

   _____

9A: Graphic Organizer

For use before Lesson 9-1

Study Skill Try to read new lessons before your teacher presents them in class. Important information is sometimes printed in **boldface** type or highlighted inside a box or with color. Pay special attention to this information.

Write your answers.

1. What is the chapter title? _____

2. How many lessons are there in this chapter? _____

3. What is the topic of the Test-Taking Strategies page? _____

4. Complete the graphic organizer below as you work through the chapter.

   • In the center, write the title of the chapter.

   • When you begin a lesson, write the lesson name in a rectangle.

   • When you complete a lesson, write a skill or key concept in a circle linked to that lesson block.

   • When you complete the chapter, use this graphic organizer to help you review.

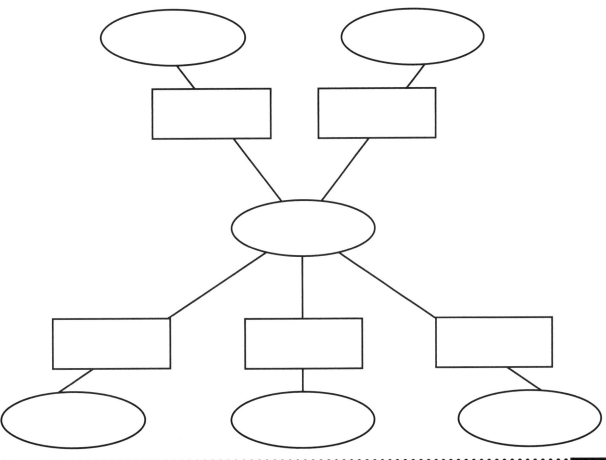

9B: Reading Comprehension

Study Skill When you complete a math exercise, always make sure your answer makes sense.

Below is an 8-day forecast of weather conditions. Use the table to answer the questions.

Date	Weather Prediction	High/Low Temp °F	% Chance of Precipitation
July 26 evening	Isolated T-Storms	67°	30%
July 27	PM T-Storms	87° / 71°	40%
July 28	Partly Cloudy	91° / 71°	20%
July 29	Scattered T-Storms	90° / 64°	40%
July 30	Partly Cloudy	87° / 65°	20%
July 31	Partly Cloudy	87° / 60°	20%
Aug 01	Partly Cloudy	83° / 59°	20%
Aug 02	Partly Cloudy	87° / 60°	0%

1. For what dates does the table give weather forecasts?

   _____

2. On which date might there be isolated thunderstorms?

   _____

3. What is the difference between the high and low temperature on August 1?

   _____

4. What is the probability of precipitation on July 30?

   _____

5. What day(s) has (have) the greatest chance for rain?

   _____

6. What are the odds *for* having rain on July 31?

   _____

7. What are the odds *against* having rain on July 29?

   _____

8. **High-Use Academic Words** What is an *exercise,* as mentioned in the study skill?

   a. something done to develop a skill   **b.** a group or set alike in some way

9C: Reading/Writing Math Symbols

Study Skill Write assignments down; do not rely only on your memory.

Write the meaning of each mathematical expression.

1. $P(A)$

   _____

2. $P(\text{not } A)$

   _____

3. $P(A, \text{then } B)$

   _____

Write each statement using appropriate mathematical symbols.

4. the probability of event C occurring

   _____

5. the probability of rolling an odd number on a number cube

   _____

6. the probability of event D, and then event E occurring

   _____

A bag contains 6 red, 2 blue, and 4 green marbles. Find each probability.

7. P(blue)

   _____

8. P(not red)

   _____

9. P(red, then blue when red is replaced)

   _____

10. P(red, then blue when red is not replaced)

   _____

9D: Visual Vocabulary Practice

For use after Lesson 9-5

High-Use Academic Words

Study Skill Mathematics is like learning a foreign language. You have to know the vocabulary before you can speak the language correctly.

Concept List

counting principle	complement	independent events
compound events	simulation	dependent events
outcome	experimental probability	sample space

Write the concept that best describes each exercise. Choose from the concept list above.

1. A model used to estimate the probability of an event. _____	**2.** A hat contains 6 names. You select 2 names without replacing the first name. _____	**3.** There are 5 marbles, 3 green and 2 red. You draw a marble, then replace it before drawing the next marble. _____
4. Two or more events _____	**5.** If you flip a coin, then flipping heads is an example of this. _____	**6.** Pedro draws a card from a standard 52-card deck. He then rolls a six-sided number cube. The total number of possible outcomes is $52 \times 6 = 312$. _____
7. $\boxed{\text{A B C}}$ In the set above, this is represented by {A, B, C}. _____	**8.** Probability that is based on observation. _____	**9.** Renee rolls a six-sided number cube. If an event represents rolling an even number, then this is represented by the set {1, 3, 5}. _____

9E: Vocabulary Check

For use after Lesson 9-5

Study Skill Strengthen your vocabulary. Use these pages and add cues and summaries by applying the Cornell Notetaking style.

Write the definition for each word or term at the right. To check your work, fold the paper back along the dotted line to see the correct answers.

_____

_____

_____

independent event

_____

_____

_____

sample space

_____

_____

_____

event

_____

_____

theoretical
probability

_____

_____

experimental
probability

_____

_____

9E: Vocabulary Check (continued)   For use after Lesson 9-5

Write the vocabulary word or term for each definition. To check your work, fold the paper forward along the dotted line to see the correct answers.

the occurrence of one event does not affect the probability of the occurrence of the other event

_____

the set of all possible outcomes of a probability experiment

_____

a collection of possible outcomes

_____

the ratio of the number of favorable outcomes to the number of possible outcomes

_____

the ratio of the number of times an event occurs to the total number of trials

_____

Name _____ Class _____ Date _____

9F: Vocabulary Review

For use with the Chapter Review

Study Skill When using a word bank, read the words first. Then answer the questions.

Complete the crossword puzzle. Use the words from the following list.

parallelogram	conjecture	decagon	equation	mode
complement	symmetry	variable	discount	prime
independent	probability	dependent	outcome	slope

DOWN

1. prediction that suggests what you expect will happen

2. difference between the original price and the sale price

3. letter that stands for a number

5. ratio that describes the steepness of a line

6. used to express how likely an event is

7. number that occurs most often in a data set

9. collection of outcomes not contained in the event

10. mathematical statement with an equal sign

12. polygon with ten sides

13. whole number with only two factors, itself and the number one

ACROSS

2. Events are _____ if the occurrence of one event affects the probability of the occurrence of another event.

4. A figure has _____ if one side of the figure is the mirror image of the other side.

6. four-sided figure with two sets of parallel lines

8. possible result of an action

11. Events are _____ if the occurrence of one event does not affect the probability of the occurrence of another event.